A more secure world:
Our shared responsibility

Report of the High-level Panel on Threats,
Challenges and Change

United Nations
2004

The United Nations gratefully acknowledges the financial support of the United Nations Foundation for the printing of this publication.

Designed by the Graphic Design Unit
United Nations Department of Public Information

Contents

Foreword by the
United Nations Secretary-General

Historians may well look back on the first years of the twenty-first century as a decisive moment in the human story. The different societies that make up the human family are today interconnected as never before. They face threats that no nation can hope to master by acting alone - and opportunities that can be much more hopefully exploited if all nations work together.

The purpose of this report is to suggest how nations *can* work together to meet this formidable challenge. It is the work of a panel of sixteen eminent and experienced people, drawn from different parts of the world, whom I asked a year ago to assess current threats to international peace and security; to evaluate how well our existing policies and institutions have done in addressing those threats; and to recommend ways of strengthening the United Nations to provide collective security for the twenty-first century.

The Panel has met, and even surpassed, my expectations. This is a report of great range and depth, which sets out a broad framework for collective security, and indeed gives a broader meaning to that concept, appropriate for the new millennium. It suggests not only ways to deal with particular threats, but also new ways of understanding the connections between them, and explains what this implies in terms of shared policies and institutions. In so doing, it also offers a unique opportunity to refashion and renew the United Nations, which world leaders defined four years ago, in the Millennium Declaration, as "the indispensable common house of the entire human family".

Findings and recommendations

I wholly endorse the report's core argument that what is needed is a comprehensive system of collective security: one that tackles both new and old threats, and addresses the security concerns of all States - rich and poor, weak and strong. Particularly important is the report's insistence that today's threats to our security are all interconnected. We can no longer afford to see problems such as terrorism, or civil wars, or extreme poverty, in isolation. Our strategies must be comprehensive. Our institutions must overcome their narrow preoccupations and learn to work across the whole range of issues, in a concerted fashion.

The report argues that the front line in today's combat must be manned by capable and responsible **States**. I agree. The task of helping States improve their own capacities to deal with contemporary threats is vital and urgent. The United Nations must be able to do this better. The Panel tells us how.

Other findings of the report that I consider particularly important include the following:

- **Development** and security are inextricably linked. A more secure world is only possible if poor countries are given a real chance to develop. Extreme poverty and infectious diseases threaten many people directly, but they also provide a fertile breeding-ground for other threats, including civil conflict. Even people in rich countries will be more secure if their Governments help poor countries to defeat poverty and disease by meeting the Millennium Development Goals.

- We need to pay much closer attention to **biological security**. Our response to HIV/AIDS was, as the report says, "shockingly late and shamefully ill-resourced", and donors are still not providing anything like the amount of aid needed to halt the pandemic. But the report goes further. It calls attention to the overall deterioration of our global health system, which is ill-equipped to protect us against existing and emerging infectious diseases; and it highlights both the promise and the peril of advances in biotechnology. It calls for a major initiative to rebuild global public health, beginning with a concerted effort to build public health capacity throughout the developing world, at both local and national levels. This will not only yield direct benefits by preventing and treating disease in the developing world itself, but will also provide the basis for an effective global defence against bio-terrorism and overwhelming natural outbreaks of deadly infectious disease.

- While our principal aim should be to prevent threats from emerging, when they do emerge we must be better prepared to **respond**. Two of the tools we have for this are **sanctions** and **mediation**. The Panel recommends ways to strengthen both. I urge Governments to adopt them.

- When all else fails, it may be necessary and legitimate to **use force**. The report makes a crucial contribution to the search for common criteria, by which to decide when the use of force is justified. I hope Governments will consider its recommendations very carefully. A new consensus on this issue is essential if our collective security system is ever to be truly effective.

- The United Nations must make better use of its assets in the fight against **terrorism**, articulating an effective and principled counter-terrorism strategy that is respectful of the rule of law and universal human rights. One of the obstacles to this up to now has been the inability of United Nations members to agree on a definition of terrorism. The report offers a definition which, I believe, will help build the consensus we need if we are to move forward quickly.

- There is a real danger that we could see a cascade of **nuclear proliferation** in the near future. The report recommends ways of strengthening the non-proliferation regime by creating incentives for States to forego the development of domestic uranium enrichment and reprocessing facililities, and calls for a voluntary time-limited moratorium on the construction of any such facilities. These suggestions, if implemented swiftly and firmly, offer us a real chance to reduce the risk of a nuclear attack, whether by States or non-State actors. They should be put into effect without delay.

- No less important are the recommendations for **adapting the United Nations for the twenty-first century**. The report criticizes several areas of the United Nations performance and - however implicitly - United Nations management, for which I take responsibility. These criticisms deserve to be taken seriously, and acted upon.

- All the United Nations principal organs are in need of change, including the Security Council. The report offers two alternative formulae for expanding the Council's membership, which I hope will make it easier for Governments to reach a decision in 2005.

- The report rightly identifies **post-conflict peacebuilding** as an area of vital concern, and offers new ideas for improving our performance in this area - including a new inter-governmental body, the 'Peacebuilding Commission', whose task would be to help States make a successful transition from the immediate post-conflict phase to longer-term reconstruction and development.

- The report also recommends changes to the **Commission on Human Rights**. The Universal Declaration of Human Rights remains one of the United Nations greatest achievements, and we should all be proud of the Organization's work in developing international human rights norms and standards. But we cannot move forward without restoring the credibility and effectiveness of our human rights mechanisms and refocusing ourselves on the protection of individual rights.

- Finally, the report makes recommendations, which I welcome, for **strengthening the Secretariat**. The world needs, and is entitled to expect, an effective United Nations Secretariat, which can attract and retain the best people from all parts of the world.

Conclusion

I hope people all over the world will read this report, discuss it, and urge their Governments to take prompt decisions on its recommendations. I believe the great majority of them will share my feeling that there is an urgent need for the nations of the world to come together and reach a new consensus - both on the future of collective security and on the changes needed if the United Nations is to play its part.

For my part, I will move quickly to consider and implement, as appropriate, those recommendations that are within my purview. I urge the other organs of the United

Nations to do the same. And on those issues - such as the rules and norms governing the use of force - which go to the very heart of who we are as the United Nations and what we stand for, I believe decisions should be taken by world leaders next September, when they meet for a special summit at United Nations Headquarters in New York. In March 2005 I shall submit a report of my own, which I hope will help to set the agenda for that summit.

Finally, I would like to express my sincere admiration for the work of the Chair and members of the Panel in producing this report. They did not shrink from tackling the toughest issues that divide us. That such a diverse group, composed of such experienced people, could reach consensus on such farsighted, yet workable, recommendations gives me hope that the nations of the world can do the same, thereby giving new meaning and resonance to the name "United Nations".

Kofi A. Annan
Secretary-General of the United Nations

Transmittal letter addressed to the Secretary-General from the Chair of the High-level Panel on Threats, Challenges and Change

I have the privilege to transmit to you the report of the High-level Panel on Threats, Challenges and Change, entitled "A more secure world: our shared responsibility."

The report puts forward a new vision of collective security, one that addresses all of the major threats to international peace and security felt around the world. Our research and consultations revealed that ours is an age of unparalleled interconnection among threats to international peace and security, and mutual vulnerability between weak and strong. We found that the United Nations has been much more effective in addressing the major threats to peace and security than it is given credit for, but that nonetheless major changes are needed if the United Nations is to be effective, efficient and equitable in providing collective security for all in the twenty-first century.

Our mandate from you precluded any in-depth examination of individual conflicts and we have respected that guidance. But the members of the Panel believe it would be remiss of them if they failed to point out that no amount of systemic changes to the way the United Nations handles both old and new threats to peace and security will enable it to discharge effectively its role under the Charter if efforts are not redoubled to resolve a number of long-standing disputes which continue to fester and to feed the new threats we now face. Foremost among these are the issues of Palestine, Kashmir and the Korean Peninsula.

The members of the Panel may not be in full agreement with every specific point and detail of the report, but they all endorse the report and generally agree with its findings. I undertake to draw to your attention, however, that the members of the Panel disagree about the models put forth for Security Council expansion and the method for determining criteria for Security Council membership. Some members of the Panel believe strongly that only the model involving expansion of permanent membership, albeit without a veto, will equip the Security Council to deal with the new century's threats. Others believe equally strongly that the alternative model involving elected, long-term but non-permanent members is the better way to proceed. We all agree, however, that it would be a major error to allow the discussions needed to move towards a decision between the two options to divert attention from decisions on the many other necessary proposals for change, the validity and viability of which do not depend on Security Council enlargement.

Our report is addressed to you, but many of our recommendations will require commitment from and action by heads of Government. Only through their leadership can we realistically forge the new consensus required to meet the threats described in our report.

Our deliberations drew on inputs from a wide range of sources, including Governments, academic experts and civil society organizations across the globe. None of our work would have been possible were it not for the extensive support we received. The following Governments made generous financial contributions to our work: Austria, Australia, Belgium, Brazil, Canada, China, Denmark, France, Greece, Ireland, Italy, Japan, Jordan, Kazakhstan, Mauritius, Netherlands, New Zealand, Norway, Portugal, Russian Federation, Singapore, South Africa, Spain, Sweden, Switzerland, Thailand, Turkey and United Kingdom. The following foundations and think tanks made financial or in-kind contributions to our work: Carnegie Corporation of New York, Ford Foundation, John D. and Catherine T. MacArthur Foundation, New York University Center on International Cooperation, Rockefeller Brothers Fund, Rockefeller Foundation, Stanford University Center for International Security and Cooperation, Stanley Foundation, United Nations Foundation and William and Flora Hewlett Foundation.

I should like to conclude by thanking you most warmly on my own behalf and that of other members of the Panel for the honour of entrusting to us this important task. I also wish to register our gratitude to all those who have contributed over the past year to our process of reflection, and above all to our Research Director, Stephen Stedman, and the Secretary of the Panel, Loraine Rickard-Martin, and their staff, without whose hard work and intellectual contributions the present report would not have seen the light of day.

Anand Panyarachun
Chairman
High-level Panel on Threats, Challenges and Change

Synopsis

Towards a new security consensus

The United Nations was created in 1945 above all else "to save succeeding generations from the scourge of war" - to ensure that the horrors of the World Wars were never repeated. Sixty years later, we know all too well that the biggest security threats we face now, and in the decades ahead, go far beyond States waging aggressive war. They extend to poverty, infectious disease and environmental degradation; war and violence within States; the spread and possible use of nuclear, radiological, chemical and biological weapons; terrorism; and transnational organized crime. The threats are from non-State actors as well as States, and to human security as well as State security.

The preoccupation of the United Nations founders was with State security. When they spoke of creating a new system of collective security they meant it in the traditional military sense: a system in which States join together and pledge that aggression against one is aggression against all, and commit themselves in that event to react collectively. But they also understood well, long before the idea of human security gained currency, the indivisibility of security, economic development and human freedom. In the opening words of the Charter, the United Nations was created "to reaffirm faith in fundamental human rights" and "to promote social progress and better standards of life in larger freedom".

The central challenge for the twenty-first century is to fashion a new and broader understanding, bringing together all these strands, of what collective security means - and of all the responsibilities, commitments, strategies and institutions that come with it if a collective security system is to be effective, efficient and equitable.

If there is to be a new security consensus, it must start with the understanding that the front-line actors in dealing with all the threats we face, new and old, continue to be individual sovereign States, whose role and responsibilities, and right to be respected, are fully recognized in the Charter of the United Nations. But in the twenty-first century, more than ever before, no State can stand wholly alone. Collective strategies, collective institutions and a sense of collective responsibility are indispensable.

The case for collective security today rests on three basic pillars. Today's threats recognize no national boundaries, are connected, and must be addressed at the global and regional as well as the national levels. No State, no matter how powerful, can by its own efforts alone make itself invulnerable to today's threats. And it cannot be assumed that every State will always be able, or willing, to meet its responsibility to protect its own peoples and not to harm its neighbours.

We must not underestimate the difficulty of reaching a new consensus about the meaning and responsibilities of collective security. Many will regard one or more of the threats we identify as not really being a threat to international peace and security. Some believe that HIV/AIDS is a horrible disease, but not a security threat. Or that terrorism is a threat to some States, but not all. Or that civil wars in Africa are a humanitarian tragedy, but surely not a problem for international security. Or that poverty is a problem of development, not security.

Differences of power, wealth and geography do determine what we perceive as the gravest threats to our survival and well-being. Differences of focus lead us to dismiss what others perceive as the gravest of all threats to their survival. Inequitable responses to threats further fuel division. Many people believe that what passes for collective security today is simply a system for protecting the rich and powerful. Such perceptions pose a fundamental challenge to building collective security today. Stated baldly, without mutual recognition of threats there can be no collective security. Self-help will rule, mistrust will predominate and cooperation for long-term mutual gain will elude us.

What is needed today is nothing less than a new consensus between alliances that are frayed, between wealthy nations and poor, and among peoples mired in mistrust across an apparently widening cultural abyss. The essence of that consensus is simple: we all share responsibility for each other's security. And the test of that consensus will be action.

Collective security and the challenge of prevention

Any event or process that leads to large-scale death or lessening of life chances and undermines States as the basic unit of the international system is a threat to international security. So defined, there are six clusters of threats with which the world must be concerned now and in the decades ahead:

- Economic and social threats, including poverty, infectious disease and environmental degradation
- Inter-State conflict
- Internal conflict, including civil war, genocide and other large-scale atrocities
- Nuclear, radiological, chemical and biological weapons
- Terrorism
- Transnational organized crime

In its first 60 years, the United Nations has made crucial contributions to reducing or mitigating these threats to international security. While there have been major failures and shortcomings, the record of successes and contributions is underappreciated. This gives hope that the Organization can adapt to successfully confront the new challenges of the twenty-first century.

The primary challenge for the United Nations and its members is to ensure that, of all the threats in the categories listed, those that are distant do not become imminent and those that are imminent do not actually become destructive. This requires a framework for preventive action which addresses all these threats in all the ways they resonate most in different parts of the world. Most of all, it will require leadership at the domestic and international levels to act early, decisively and collectively against all these threats - from HIV/AIDS to nuclear terrorism - before they have their most devastating effect.

In describing how to meet the challenge of prevention, we begin with development because it is the indispensable foundation for a collective security system that takes prevention seriously. It serves multiple functions. It helps combat the poverty, infectious disease and environmental degradation that kill millions and threaten human security. It is vital in helping States prevent or reverse the erosion of State capacity, which is crucial for meeting almost every class of threat. And it is part of a long-term strategy for preventing civil war and for addressing the environments in which both terrorism and organized crime flourish.

Collective security and the use of force

What happens if peaceful prevention fails? If none of the preventive measures so far described stop the descent into war and chaos? If distant threats do become imminent? Or if imminent threats become actual? Or if a non-imminent threat nonetheless becomes very real and measures short of the use of military force seem powerless to stop it?

We address here the circumstances in which effective collective security may require the backing of military force, starting with the rules of international law that must govern any decision to go to war if anarchy is not to prevail. It is necessary to distinguish between situations in which a State claims to act in self-defence; situations in which a State is posing a threat to others outside its borders; and situations in which the threat is primarily internal and the issue is the responsibility to protect a State's own people. In all cases, we believe that the Charter of the United Nations, properly understood and applied, is equal to the task: Article 51 needs neither extension nor restriction of its long-understood scope, and Chapter VII fully empowers the Security Council to deal with every kind of threat that States may confront. The task is not to find alternatives to the Security Council as a source of authority but to make it work better than it has.

That force *can* legally be used does not always mean that, as a matter of good conscience and good sense, it *should* be used. We identify a set of guidelines - five criteria of legitimacy - which we believe that the Security Council (and anyone else involved in these decisions) should always address in considering whether to authorize or apply military force. The adoption of these guidelines (seriousness of threat, proper purpose, last resort, proportional means and balance of consequences) will not produce agreed conclusions with push-button predictability, but should significantly improve the chances of reaching international consensus on what have been in recent years deeply divisive issues.

We also address here the other major issues that arise during and after violent conflict, including the needed capacities for peace enforcement, peacekeeping and peacebuilding, and the protection of civilians. A central recurring theme is the necessity for all members of the international community, developed and developing States alike, to be much more forthcoming in providing and supporting deployable military resources. Empty gestures are all too easy to make: an effective, efficient and equitable collective security system demands real commitment.

A more effective United Nations for the twenty-first century

The United Nations was never intended to be a utopian exercise. It was meant to be a collective security system that worked. The Charter of the United Nations provided the most powerful States with permanent membership on the Security Council and the veto. In exchange, they were expected to use their power for the common good and promote and obey international law. As Harry Truman, then President of the United States, noted in his speech to the final plenary session of the founding conference of the United Nations Organization, "we all have to recognize - no matter how great our strength - that we must deny ourselves the licence to do always as we please".

In approaching the issue of United Nations reform, it is as important today as it was in 1945 to combine power with principle. Recommendations that ignore underlying power realities will be doomed to failure or irrelevance, but recommendations that simply reflect raw distributions of power and make no effort to bolster international principles are unlikely to gain the widespread adherence required to shift international behaviour.

Proposed changes should be driven by real-world need. Change for its own sake is likely to run the well-worn course of the endless reform debates of the past decade. The litmus test is this: does a proposed change help meet the challenge posed by a virulent threat?

Throughout the work of the High-level Panel on Threats, Challenges and Change, we have looked for institutional weaknesses in current responses to threats. The following stand as the most urgently in need of remedy:

- The General Assembly has lost vitality and often fails to focus effectively on the most compelling issues of the day.
- The Security Council will need to be more proactive in the future. For this to happen, those who contribute most to the Organization financially, militarily

and diplomatically should participate more in Council decision-making, and those who participate in Council decision-making should contribute more to the Organization. The Security Council needs greater credibility, legitimacy and representation to do all that we demand of it.

- There is a major institutional gap in addressing countries under stress and countries emerging from conflict. Such countries often suffer from attention, policy guidance and resource deficits.
- The Security Council has not made the most of the potential advantages of working with regional and subregional organizations.
- There must be new institutional arrangements to address the economic and social threats to international security.
- The Commission on Human Rights suffers from a legitimacy deficit that casts doubts on the overall reputation of the United Nations.
- There is a need for a more professional and better organized Secretariat that is much more capable of concerted action.

The reforms we propose will not by themselves make the United Nations more effective. In the absence of Member States reaching agreement on the security consensus contained in the present report, the United Nations will underachieve. Its institutions will still only be as strong as the energy, resources and attention devoted to them by Member States and their leaders.

Part 1
Towards a new security consensus

Part 1
Towards a new security consensus

Synopsis

The United Nations was created in 1945 above all else "to save succeeding generations from the scourge of war" - to ensure that the horrors of the World Wars were never repeated. Sixty years later, we know all too well that the biggest security threats we face now, and in the decades ahead, go far beyond States waging aggressive war. They extend to poverty, infectious disease and environmental degradation; war and violence within States; the spread and possible use of nuclear, radiological, chemical and biological weapons; terrorism; and transnational organized crime. The threats are from non-State actors as well as States, and to human security as well as State security.

The preoccupation of the United Nations founders was with State security. When they spoke of creating a new system of collective security they meant it in the traditional military sense: a system in which States join together and pledge that aggression against one is aggression against all, and commit themselves in that event to react collectively. But they also understood well, long before the idea of human security gained currency, the indivisibility of security, economic development and human freedom. In the opening words of the Charter, the United Nations was created "to reaffirm faith in fundamental human rights" and "to promote social progress and better standards of life in larger freedom".

The central challenge for the twenty-first century is to fashion a new and broader understanding, bringing together all these strands, of what collective security means - and of all the responsibilities, commitments, strategies and institutions that come with it if a collective security system is to be effective, efficient and equitable:

If there is to be a new security consensus, it must start with the understanding that the front-line actors in dealing with all the threats we face, new and old, continue to be individual sovereign States, whose role and responsibilities, and right to be respected, are fully recognized in the Charter of the United Nations. But in the twenty-first century, more than ever before, no State can stand wholly alone. Collective strategies, collective institutions and a sense of collective responsibility are indispensable.

The case for collective security today rests on three basic pillars. Today's threats recognize no national boundaries, are connected, and must be addressed at the global and regional as well as national levels. No State, no matter how powerful, can by its own efforts alone make itself invulnerable to today's threats. And it cannot be assumed that every State will always be able, or willing, to meet its responsibility to protect its own peoples and not to harm its neighbours.

We must not underestimate the difficulty of reaching a new consensus about the meaning and responsibilities of collective security. Many will regard one or more of the threats we identify as not really being a threat to international peace and security. Some believe that HIV/AIDS is a horrible disease, but not a security threat. Or that terrorism is a threat to some States, but not all. Or that civil wars in Africa are a humanitarian tragedy, but surely not a problem for international security. Or that poverty is a problem of development, not security.

Differences of power, wealth and geography do determine what we perceive as the gravest threats to our survival and well-being. Differences of focus lead us to dismiss what others perceive as the gravest of all threats to their survival. Inequitable responses to threats further fuel division. Many people believe that what passes for collective security today is simply a system for protecting the rich and powerful. Such perceptions pose a fundamental challenge to building collective security today. Stated baldly, without mutual recognition of threats there can be no collective security. Self-help will rule, mistrust will predominate and cooperation for long-term mutual gain will elude us.

What is needed today is nothing less than a new consensus between alliances that are frayed, between wealthy nations and poor, and among peoples mired in mistrust across an apparently widening cultural abyss. The essence of that consensus is simple: we all share responsibility for each other's security. And the test of that consensus will be action.

I. Different worlds: 1945 and 2005

1.   The United Nations was created in a spirit of optimism fuelled by the end of the Second World War and the will to avoid a repeat of its horrors and those of its predecessor. For many of the States most traumatized by two world wars, the experiment has been successful. Over the subsequent 60 years, many parts of the world have enjoyed unparalleled peace and prosperity. The dynamics and tensions that led to the Second World War were laid to rest, war between the great Powers was avoided and a stable peace emerged in Europe. Japan, Germany and Italy were successfully integrated into the family of nations and are currently the second, third and sixth largest financial contributors to the United Nations.

2.   In the first 30 years of the United Nations, dozens of new States emerged from colonial systems that, until recent times, tied half of mankind to a handful of capitals. Assisting new States into being was a seminal contribution of the United Nations during this period. Decolonization in turn transformed the United Nations. At the creation of the United Nations in 1945, there were 51 members; today there are 191. The General Assembly was transformed from a body composed of States that largely resembled one another to one whose membership varied dramatically. By the mid-1960s, developing countries

formed a majority in the General Assembly and through it gained a voice in international politics largely denied to them outside the institution.

3.   The second half of the twentieth century was a struggle for the viability of these new States and the well-being of their citizens. They inherited arbitrary colonial boundaries and colonial economies designed to serve the needs of the metropole. Independence was the start of a race to educate and develop the professional, scientific and technological expertise to run modern States and economies. All of this took place in an era of huge expectations about what States could and should deliver, when most models of economic growth relied on heavy State control.

4.   In the last 40 years, life expectancy in developing countries has increased by 20 years, and per capita income has doubled in such countries as Botswana, Brazil, China, the Republic of Korea and Turkey in less than a third of the time it took to do so in the United Kingdom or the United States a century or more earlier. Despite such progress, however, large parts of the world remained mired in life-threatening poverty. Between 1975 and 1999, sub-Saharan Africa saw no overall increase in its per capita income.

5.   By the 1980s, many of these new States faced crises of State capacity and legitimacy, reflected in the rise of internal wars as the dominant form of warfare in the second half of the twentieth century (see figure below).

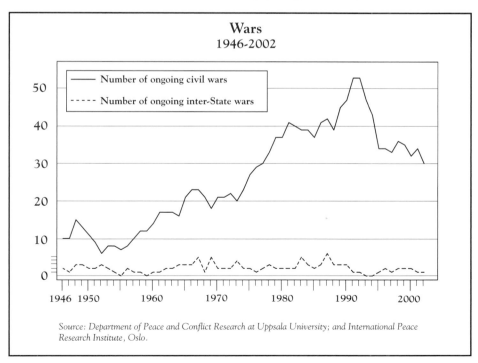

Wars
1946-2002

——— Number of ongoing civil wars

- - - - - Number of ongoing inter-State wars

Source: Department of Peace and Conflict Research at Uppsala University; and International Peace Research Institute, Oslo.

6.   As we enter the twenty-first century, these struggles are far from over. More than a billion people lack access to clean water, more than two billion have no access to adequate sanitation and more than three million die every year from water-related diseases. Fourteen million people, including six million children, die every year from hunger. There were 842 million undernourished people in 2000; 95 per cent lived in poor countries.

7.   Almost 30 million people in Africa now have HIV/AIDS. In the worst-affected States, middle-aged urban elites are heavily afflicted, eroding State capacity and decimating the economic activity of what should be a State's most productive group. The increasing number of infected women and girls is threatening food and agricultural production. If trends are not reversed, some of these States face collapse under the combined weight of poverty and HIV/AIDS.

8.   Decolonization was only one of the forces that shaped the United Nations. The United Nations founders did not anticipate that the United States and the former Soviet Union would soon embark on a global rivalry, developing and deploying tens of thousands of nuclear weapons capable of destroying the world many times over.

9.   Controlling the destructive capability of nuclear technology and harnessing its promise became central to the work of the United Nations. The very first resolution adopted by the General Assembly in 1946 called for the disarmament of "weapons adaptable to mass destruction".

10.   The cold war shaped much of global politics for the next 45 years. The rivalry between the United States and the former Soviet Union blocked the Security Council from playing a dominant role in maintaining international peace and security. Nearly all armed conflicts and struggles for liberation were viewed through the prism of East-West rivalry until the historic collapse of the former Soviet Union and the end of communist rule in Eastern Europe.

11.   Nonetheless, without the United Nations the post-1945 world would very probably have been a bloodier place. There were fewer inter-State wars in the last half of the twentieth century than in the first half. Given that during the same period the number of States grew almost fourfold, one might have expected to see a marked rise in inter-State wars. Yet that did not occur and the United Nations contributed to that result. The United Nations diminished the threat of inter-State war in several ways. Peace was furthered by the invention of peacekeeping; diplomacy was carried out by the Secretary-General; disputes were remedied under the International Court of Justice; and a strong norm was upheld against aggressive war.

12.   The dramatic but peaceful end of the cold war opened an opportunity for collective security to flourish. The first years after the end of the cold war seemed to point towards a new role for the United Nations. In 1990, the Security

Council authorized the use of force against Iraq to liberate Kuwait. The Security Council broadened the interpretation of threats to international peace and security to authorize an intervention for humanitarian purposes in Somalia. The United Nations helped bring to an end several protracted wars in Central America and Southern Africa.

13. The moment was short-lived. It quickly became apparent that the United Nations had exchanged the shackles of the cold war for the straitjacket of Member State complacency and great Power indifference. Although the United Nations gave birth to the notion of human security, it proved poorly equipped to provide it. Long-standing regional conflicts, such as those involving Israel/Palestine and Kashmir, remained unresolved. Failures to act in the face of ethnic cleansing and genocide in Rwanda and Bosnia eroded international support. Optimism yielded to renewed cynicism about the willingness of Member States to support the Organization.

> *The attacks of 11 September 2001 revealed that States, as well as collective security institutions, have failed to keep pace with changes in the nature of threats.*

14. The terrorist attacks of 11 September 2001 on New York and Washington, D.C., brought with them a glimpse of the potential for renewed collective security. On 12 September 2001, France introduced and the Security Council unanimously passed resolution 1368 (2001), which condemned the attacks and opened the way for United States-led military action against the Taliban regime in self-defence. On the same day, the General Assembly condemned terrorism and the attacks. On 28 September 2001, the Security Council adopted resolution 1373 (2001), which obligates all Member States, under Chapter VII of the Charter of the United Nations, to take specific actions to combat terrorism. Three months later, the United Nations presided over the Bonn Agreement, which created an interim government to replace the deposed Taliban regime. The United Nations stood behind the interim government in Afghanistan as custodian of the peace process and helped to draft the country's new constitution.

15. This spirit of international purpose lasted only months and was eroded by divisions over the United States-led war in Iraq in 2003.

16. The attacks of 11 September 2001 revealed that States, as well as collective security institutions, have failed to keep pace with changes in the nature of threats. The technological revolution that has radically changed the worlds of communication, information-processing, health and transportation has eroded borders, altered migration and allowed individuals the world over to share information at a speed inconceivable two decades ago. Such changes have brought many benefits but also great potential for harm. Smaller and smaller

numbers of people are able to inflict greater and greater amounts of damage, without the support of any State. A new threat, transnational organized crime, undermines the rule of law within and across borders. Technologies designed to improve daily life can be transformed into instruments of aggression. We have yet to fully understand the impact of these changes, but they herald a fundamentally different security climate - one whose unique opportunities for cooperation are matched by an unprecedented scope for destruction.

Today, more than ever before, a threat to one is a threat to all. The mutual vulnerability of weak and strong has never been clearer.

II. The case for comprehensive collective security

A. Threats without boundaries

17.   Today, more than ever before, threats are interrelated and a threat to one is a threat to all. The mutual vulnerability of weak and strong has never been clearer.

18.   Global economic integration means that a major terrorist attack anywhere in the developed world would have devastating consequences for the well-being of millions of people in the developing world. The World Bank estimates that the attacks of 11 September 2001 alone increased the number of people living in poverty by 10 million; the total cost to the world economy probably exceeded 80 billion dollars. These numbers would be far surpassed by an incident involving nuclear terrorism.

19.   Similarly, the security of the most affluent State can be held hostage to the ability of the poorest State to contain an emerging disease. Because international flight times are shorter than the incubation periods for many infectious diseases, any one of 700 million international airline passengers every year can be an unwitting global disease-carrier. Severe acute respiratory syndrome (SARS) spread to more than 8,000 people in 30 countries in three months, killing almost 700. The influenza pandemic of 1919 killed as many as 100 million people, far more than the First World War, over a period of a little more than a year. Today, a similar virus could kill tens of millions in a fraction of the time.

20.   Every threat to international security today enlarges the risk of other threats. Nuclear proliferation by States increases the availability of the materiel and technology necessary for a terrorist to acquire a nuclear weapon. The ability of non-State actors to traffic in nuclear materiel and technology is aided by ineffective State control of borders and transit through weak States.

21.   International terrorist groups prey on weak States for sanctuary. Their recruitment is aided by grievances nurtured by poverty, foreign occupation and the

absence of human rights and democracy; by religious and other intolerance; and by civil violence - a witch's brew common to those areas where civil war and regional conflict intersect. In recent years, terrorists have helped to finance their activities and moved large sums of money by gaining access to such valuable commodities as drugs in countries beset by civil war.

22.   Poverty, infectious disease, environmental degradation and war feed one another in a deadly cycle. Poverty (as measured by per capita gross domestic product (GDP)) is strongly associated with the outbreak of civil war (see figure below). Such diseases as malaria and HIV/AIDS continue to cause large numbers of deaths and reinforce poverty. Disease and poverty, in turn, are connected to environmental degradation; climate change exacerbates the occurrence of such infectious disease as malaria and dengue fever. Environmental stress, caused by large populations and shortages of land and other natural resources, can contribute to civil violence.

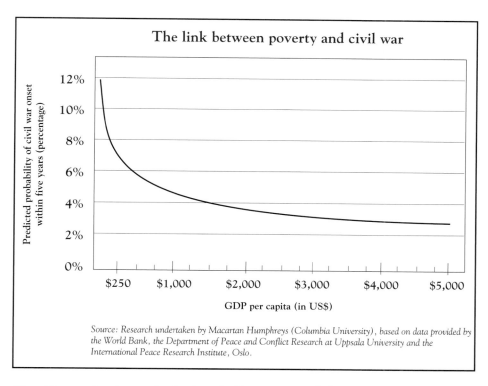

The link between poverty and civil war

Source: Research undertaken by Macartan Humphreys (Columbia University), based on data provided by the World Bank, the Department of Peace and Conflict Research at Uppsala University and the International Peace Research Institute, Oslo.

23.   Transnational organized crime facilitates many of the most serious threats to international peace and security. Corruption, illicit trade and money-laundering contribute to State weakness, impede economic growth and undermine democracy. These activities thus create a permissive environment for civil conflict. The prospect of organized criminal groups providing nuclear, radiological, chemical and biological weapon to terrorists is particularly worrying. Increasing drug

trade partly accounts for rapidly increasing levels of HIV/AIDS infections, especially in Eastern Europe and parts of Asia. And organized criminal activities undermine peacebuilding efforts and fuel many civil wars through illicit trade in conflict commodities and small arms.

B. The limits of self-protection

24. No State, no matter how powerful, can by its own efforts alone make itself invulnerable to today's threats. Every State requires the cooperation of other States to make itself secure. It is in every State's interest, accordingly, to cooperate with other States to address their most pressing threats, because doing so will maximize the chances of reciprocal cooperation to address its own threat priorities.

25. Take, as one example, the threat of nuclear terrorism. Experts estimate that terrorists with 50 kilograms of highly enriched uranium (HEU), an amount that would fit into six one-litre milk cartons, need only smuggle it across borders in order to create an improvised nuclear device that could level a medium-sized city. Border controls will not provide adequate defence against this threat. To overcome the threat of nuclear terrorism requires the cooperation of States, strong and weak, to clean up stockpiles of HEU, better protect shipping containers at ports and agree on new rules regulating the enrichment of uranium. Cooperation in the sharing of intelligence by States is essential for stopping terrorism.

26. Similarly, in order to stop organized crime States must cooperate to fight money-laundering, trafficking in drugs and persons, and corruption. International efforts to stem the problem are only as strong as the weakest link. Ineffective collective security institutions diminish the security of every region and State.

27. The most robust defence against the possible terrorist use of nuclear, chemical or biological weapons would seek to control dangerous materials, deter and capture terrorists, and address the broader threats that increase the risk of terrorist action. Civil war, disease and poverty increase the likelihood of State collapse and facilitate the spread of organized crime, thus also increasing the risk of terrorism and proliferation due to weak States and weak collective capacity to exercise the rule of law. Preventing mass-casualty terrorism requires a deep engagement to strengthen collective security systems, ameliorate poverty, combat extremism, end the grievances that flow from war, tackle the spread of infectious disease and fight organized crime.

28. Thus all States have an interest in forging a new comprehensive collective security system that will commit all of them to act cooperatively in the face of a broad array of threats.

C. Sovereignty and responsibility

29. In signing the Charter of the United Nations, States not only benefit from the privileges of sovereignty but also accept its responsibilities. Whatever perceptions may have prevailed when the Westphalian system first gave rise to the notion of State sovereignty, today it clearly carries with it the obligation of a State to protect the welfare of its own peoples and meet its obligations to the wider international community. But history teaches us all too clearly that it cannot be assumed that every State will always be able, or willing, to meet its responsibilities to protect its own people and avoid harming its neighbours. And in those circumstances, the principles of collective security mean that some portion of those responsibilities should be taken up by the international community, acting in accordance with the Charter of the United Nations and the Universal Declaration of Human Rights, to help build the necessary capacity or supply the necessary protection, as the case may be.

30. What we seek to protect reflects what we value. The Charter of the United Nations seeks to protect all States, not because they are intrinsically good but because they are necessary to achieve the dignity, justice, worth and safety of their citizens. These are the values that should be at the heart of any collective security system for the twenty-first century, but too often States have failed to respect and promote them. The collective security we seek to build today asserts a shared responsibility on the part of all States and international institutions, and those who lead them, to do just that.

D. Elements of a credible collective security system

31. To be credible and sustainable a collective security system must be effective, efficient and equitable. In all these respects, the multilateral system as we now know it, in responding to the major security threats which the world has confronted in recent decades, has shown that it can perform. But it must be strengthened to perform better - in all the ways we spell out in the present report.

1. Effectiveness

32. Whether by reducing the demand for nuclear weapons, mediating inter-State conflict or ending civil wars, collective security institutions have made critical contributions to the maintenance of international peace and security, although those contributions are often denigrated, both by those who would have the institutions do more and by those who would have them do less.

33. Collective security institutions are rarely effective in isolation. Multilateral institutions normally operate alongside national, regional and sometimes civil

society actors, and are most effective when these efforts are aligned to common goals. This is as true of mediation as it is of post-conflict reconstruction, poverty-reduction strategies and non-proliferation measures.

34. States are still the front-line responders to today's threats. Successful international actions to battle poverty, fight infectious disease, stop transnational crime, rebuild after civil war, reduce terrorism and halt the spread of dangerous materials all require capable, responsible States as partners. It follows that greater effort must be made to enhance the capacity of States to exercise their sovereignty responsibly. For all those in a position to help others build that capacity, it should be part of their responsibility to do so.

> *Monitoring and verification work best when they are treated as complements to, not substitutes for, enforcement.*

35. Collective action often fails, sometimes dramatically so. Collective instruments are often hampered by a lack of compliance, erratic monitoring and verification, and weak enforcement. Early warning is only effective when it leads to early action for prevention. Monitoring and verification work best when they are treated as complements to, not substitutes for, enforcement.

36. Collective security institutions have proved particularly poor at meeting the challenge posed by large-scale, gross human rights abuses and genocide. This is a normative challenge to the United Nations: the concept of State and international responsibility to protect civilians from the effects of war and human rights abuses has yet to truly overcome the tension between the competing claims of sovereign inviolability and the right to intervene. It is also an operational challenge: the challenge of stopping a Government from killing its own civilians requires considerable military deployment capacity.

2. Efficiency

37. Some collective security instruments have been efficient. As the institutional embodiment of the Treaty on the Non-Proliferation of Nuclear Weapons and of considerable long-term success in preventing widespread proliferation of nuclear weapons, the International Atomic Energy Agency (IAEA) - with its regular budget of less than $275 million - stands out as an extraordinary bargain. Similarly, the Secretary-General's mediation efforts, though grossly underresourced, have helped reduce international tensions.

38. But more collective security instruments have been inefficient. Post-conflict operations, for example, have too often been characterized by countless ill-coordinated and overlapping bilateral and United Nations programmes, with inter-agency competition preventing the best use of scarce resources.

39. The biggest source of inefficiency in our collective security institutions has simply been an unwillingness to get serious about preventing deadly violence. The

failure to invest time and resources early in order to prevent the outbreak and escalation of conflicts leads to much larger and deadlier conflagrations that are much costlier to handle later.

3. Equity

40. The credibility of any system of collective security also depends on how well it promotes security for all its members, without regard to the nature of would-be beneficiaries, their location, resources or relationship to great Powers.

41. Too often, the United Nations and its Member States have discriminated in responding to threats to international security. Contrast the swiftness with which the United Nations responded to the attacks on 11 September 2001 with its actions when confronted with a far more deadly event: from April to mid-July 1994, Rwanda experienced the equivalent of three 11 September 2001 attacks every day for 100 days, all in a country whose population was one thirty-sixth that of the United States. Two weeks into the genocide, the Security Council withdrew most of its peacekeepers from the country. It took almost a month for United Nations officials to call it a genocide and even longer for some Security Council members. When a new mission was finally authorized for Rwanda, six weeks into the genocide, few States offered soldiers. The mission deployed as the genocide ended.

> *The credibility of any system of collective security also depends on how well it promotes security for all its members, without regard to the nature of would-be beneficiaries, their location, resources or relationship to great Powers.*

42. Similarly, throughout the deliberation of the High-level Panel on Threats, Challenges and Change, we have been struck once again by the glacial speed at which our institutions have responded to massive human rights violations in Darfur, Sudan.

43. When the institutions of collective security respond in an ineffective and inequitable manner, they reveal a much deeper truth about which threats matter. Our institutions of collective security must not just assert that a threat to one is truly a threat to all, but perform accordingly.

Part 2
Collective security and the challenge of prevention

Part 2
Collective security and the challenge of prevention

Synopsis

Any event or process that leads to large-scale death or lessening of life chances and undermines States as the basic unit of the international system is a threat to international security. So defined, there are six clusters of threats with which the world must be concerned now and in the decades ahead:

- Economic and social threats, including poverty, infectious disease and environmental degradation
- Inter-State conflict
- Internal conflict, including civil war, genocide and other large-scale atrocities
- Nuclear, radiological, chemical and biological weapons
- Terrorism
- Transnational organized crime

In its first 60 years, the United Nations has made crucial contributions to reducing or mitigating these threats to international security. While there have been major failures and shortcomings, the record of successes and contributions is underappreciated. This gives hope that the Organization can adapt to successfully confront the new challenges of the twenty-first century.

The primary challenge for the United Nations and its members is to ensure that, of all the threats in the categories listed, those that are distant do not become imminent and those that are imminent do not actually become destructive. This requires a framework for preventive action which addresses all these threats in all the ways they resonate most in different parts of the world. Most of all, it will require leadership at the domestic and international levels to act early, decisively and collectively against all these threats - from HIV/AIDS to nuclear terrorism - before they have their most devastating effect.

In describing how to meet the challenge of prevention, we begin with development because it is the indispensable foundation for a collective security system that takes prevention seriously. It serves multiple functions. It helps combat the poverty, infectious disease and environmental degradation that kill millions and threaten human security. It is vital in helping States prevent or reverse the erosion of State capacity, which is crucial for meeting almost every class of threat. And it is part of a long-term strategy for preventing civil war, and for addressing the environments in which both terrorism and organized crime flourish.

III. Poverty, infectious disease and environmental degradation

A. The threats we face

44. Since 1990, while developing countries' per capita income has increased an average of 3 per cent annually, the number of people living in extreme poverty has increased in some regions by more than 100 million people. In at least 54 countries, average per capita income has declined over the same period. Every year, almost 11 million children die from preventable diseases and more than half a million women die during pregnancy or childbirth. Increasing poverty is accompanied by an increase in global inequality and income inequality in many poor countries. In parts of Latin America, for example, the income of the wealthiest fifth of households is 30 times greater than that of the poorest fifth. Worldwide, women and youth are disproportionately poor.

45. When poverty is added to ethnic or regional inequalities, the grievances that stoke civil violence are compounded. While it may not reach the level of war, the combination of a surging youth population, poverty, urbanization and unemployment has resulted in increased gang violence in many cities of the developing world. As one woman poignantly asked during the Panel's consultation with civil society organizations in Africa, "How have we let what should be our greatest asset, youth, become a threat to our security?"

International response to HIV/AIDS was shockingly slow and remains shamefully ill-resourced.

46. The continent hardest hit by poverty is Africa. In sub-Saharan Africa, average life expectancy has declined from 50 to 46 since 1990. Whereas in the developed world less than one in 100 children die before age five, in most of sub-Saharan Africa that number is one in 10, and in 14 countries it is one in five. In sub-Saharan Africa, the number of people living on less than $1 a day has increased since 1990. While undernourishment decreased worldwide in the 1990s, it increased in Africa.

47. Over the past three decades, the world has seen the emergence of new infectious diseases, a resurgence of older diseases and a spread of resistance to a growing number of mainstay antibiotic drugs. Recent outbreaks of polio threaten to undermine its near eradication, which was one of the great accomplishments of the twentieth century. These trends signify a dramatic decay in local and global public health capacity.

48. International response to HIV/AIDS was shockingly slow and remains shamefully ill-resourced. The first major international initiative on HIV/AIDS, the

Global Programme on AIDS, came only in 1987, six years after the first cases of HIV were identified and after it had infected millions of people worldwide. Nine years and 25 million infections later, the Joint United Nations Programme on HIV/AIDS (UNAIDS) was created to coordinate United Nations agencies working on HIV/AIDS. By 2000, when the Security Council first discussed HIV/AIDS as a threat to international peace and security, the number of deaths per year from HIV/AIDS in Africa had outstripped the number of battle deaths in all the civil wars fought in the 1990s. By 2003, when the Global Fund to Fight AIDS, Tuberculosis and Malaria was created, there were more than 11 million children orphaned by HIV/AIDS in Africa.

49.   That Africa has borne the brunt of the HIV/AIDS pandemic raises the troubling question of whether international response would have been so slow if the disease had reduced life expectancy by 30 years in non-African countries.

50.   Progress in stemming other lethal infectious diseases remains elusive. The global drive to control tuberculosis has shown significant advances, including improvements in political commitment, financing, strategy formulation, access to medication and medical research. Yet more than 8.5 million new cases of tuberculosis emerge and more than two million people die of tuberculosis every year. The World Health Organization (WHO) estimates that, if current trends continue, between now and 2020 nearly one billion people will be newly infected, 150 million will develop the disease and 36 million will die. Further improvements in the affordability and accessibility of medicines - not just for tuberculosis - are still sorely needed.

51.   The recent international experience in combating SARS shows how the spread of infectious disease can be limited when effective global institutions work in close partnership with capable national institutions. Rapid response by WHO and national agencies contained the spread of the disease and prevented a far more serious outbreak that could have threatened thousands of lives on several continents. No State could have achieved this degree of containment of the disease in isolation.

52.   Current trends indicate persistent and possibly worsening food insecurity in many countries, especially in sub-Saharan Africa. Population growth in the developing world and increased per capita consumption in the industrialized world have led to greater demand for scarce resources. The loss of arable land, water scarcity, overfishing, deforestation and the alteration of ecosystems pose daunting challenges for sustainable development. The world's population is expected to increase from 6.3 billion today to 8.9 billion in 2050, with nearly all of that growth occurring in the countries least equipped to absorb it. Feeding such a rapidly growing population will only be possible if agricultural yields can be increased significantly and sustainably.

53.   Environmental degradation has enhanced the destructive potential of natural disasters and in some cases hastened their occurrence. The dramatic increase in major disasters witnessed in the last 50 years provides worrying evidence of this trend. More than two billion people were affected by such disasters in the last decade, and in the same period the economic toll surpassed that of the previous four decades combined. If climate change produces more acute flooding, heat waves, droughts and storms, this pace may accelerate.

54.   Rarely are environmental concerns factored into security, development or humanitarian strategies. Nor is there coherence in environmental protection efforts at the global level. Most attempts to create governance structures to tackle the problems of global environmental degradation have not effectively addressed climate change, deforestation and desertification. Regional and global multilateral treaties on the environment are undermined by inadequate implementation and enforcement by the Member States.

International institutions and States continue to treat poverty, disease and environmental degradation as stand-alone threats.

55.   International institutions and States have not organized themselves to address the problems of development in a coherent, integrated way, and instead continue to treat poverty, infectious disease and environmental degradation as stand-alone threats. The fragmented sectoral approaches of international institutions mirror the fragmented sectoral approaches of Governments: for example, finance ministries tend to work only with the international financial institutions, development ministers only with development programmes, ministers of agriculture only with food programmes and environment ministers only with environmental agencies. Bilateral donors correctly call for better United Nations coordination but show little enthusiasm for similar efforts on their own account.

56.   Existing global economic and social governance structures are woefully inadequate for the challenges ahead. To tackle the challenges of sustainable development countries must negotiate across different sectors and issues, including foreign aid, technology, trade, financial stability and development policy. Such packages are difficult to negotiate and require high-level attention and leadership from those countries that have the largest economic impacts. At the moment, there is no high-level forum which provides leaders from large industrial and developing economies a regular opportunity for frank dialogue, deliberation and problem-solving.

57.   The United Nations comparative advantage in addressing economic and social threats is its unparalleled convening power, which allows it to formulate common development targets and rally the international community around a consensus for achieving them. In recent years, the World Summit on Sustainable

Development held in Johannesburg, South Africa, and the International Conference on Financing for Development, held in Monterrey, Mexico, have led to global understanding and ambitious programmes for alleviating poverty, providing food security, growing economies and protecting the environment in ways that benefit future generations. The United Nations Millennium Declaration contains an ambitious but feasible set of agreed targets and benchmarks, later consolidated into the Millennium Development Goals, ranging from halving extreme poverty and protecting the environment to achieving greater gender equality and halting and reversing the spread of HIV/AIDS by 2015.

58. In 2002, world leaders agreed at Monterrey that aid donors and aid recipients both have obligations to achieve development. The primary responsibility for economic and social development lies with Governments, which must create a conducive environment for vigorous private-sector-led growth and aid effectiveness by pursuing sound economic policies, building effective and responsible institutions and investing in public and social services that will reach all of their people. In return for substantive improvements in the policies and institutions of developing countries, donor nations agreed to renew their efforts to reduce poverty, including by reducing trade barriers, increasing development assistance and providing debt relief for highly indebted poor countries.

B. Meeting the challenge of prevention

1. More resources and action

59. With the adoption of the Millennium Development Goals in 2000, the international community committed itself to dramatically reduce poverty by 2015. Assessments by the Millennium Project indicate that, while some regions of the world are on track to reduce by half the proportion of people living on less than $1 a day, other regions have regressed. In the area of reducing child mortality and increasing primary education enrolment, the world continues to lag behind its commitments. Little has been done to address the gender aspects of the Millennium Development Goals. Although poor and rich countries have pledged to take action to address social and economic threats, pledges have not materialized into resources and action and long-term commitments are scant. **All States must recommit themselves to the goals of eradicating poverty, achieving sustained economic growth and promoting sustainable development**.

60. We believe that the Millennium Development Goals should be placed at the centre of national and international poverty-reduction strategies. The dramatic shortfall in resources required to meet the Millennium Development Goals must be redressed, and the commitments to sound policies and good govern-

ance at all levels must be fulfilled. For the least developed countries, official development assistance (ODA) will be crucial and should be structured to support countries' Millennium Development Goal-based poverty reduction strategies. **The many donor countries which currently fall short of the United Nations 0.7 per cent gross national product (GNP) target for ODA should establish a timetable for reaching it.**

61. After years of debate on *whether* to develop innovative approaches to financing for development, such as the International Financial Facility, donors have shifted to discussions of how to do so. We welcome this and encourage donors to move quickly to decisions on this issue.

62. In Monterrey and Johannesburg, leaders agreed that poverty alleviation is undermined by continuing inequities in the global trading system. Seventy per cent of the world's poor live in rural areas and earn their income from agriculture. They pay a devastating cost when developed countries impose trade barriers on agricultural imports and subsidize agricultural exports. In 2001, the World Trade Organization (WTO) Doha Declaration explicitly committed signatories to put the needs and interests of developing countries at the heart of negotiations over a new trade round. **WTO members should strive to conclude the Doha development round at the latest in 2006.**

63. Governance reforms and improvements in trading opportunities will not by themselves bring about meaningful poverty alleviation in a significant number of the least developed countries - many of them in sub-Saharan Africa - where development efforts are undermined by poor infrastructure, low productivity agriculture, endemic disease and crippling levels of external debt. Developed countries will also have to do more to address the challenge in the poorest countries of debt sustainability - which should be redefined as the level of debt consistent with achieving the Millennium Development Goals. **Lender Governments and the international financial institutions should provide highly indebted poor countries with greater debt relief, longer rescheduling and improved access to global markets.**

64. Despite major international initiatives, the spread of HIV/AIDS is still rampant. In the most affected countries of sub-Saharan Africa, the impact of the pandemic is becoming more acute. In Asia, the number of infections exceeds seven million and is increasing rapidly. **Although international resources devoted to meeting the challenge of HIV/AIDS have increased from about $250 million in 1996 to about $2.8 billion in 2002, more than $10 billion annually is needed to stem the pandemic.**

65. The experience of some countries shows that properly funded and institutionalized efforts can yield remarkable successes in the fight against HIV/AIDS. By contrast,

where Governments have refused to acknowledge the gravity of the threat and failed to address the problem, countries have experienced a dramatic turn for the worse and international efforts to address the problem have been hampered. **Leaders of affected countries need to mobilize resources, commit funds and engage civil society and the private sector in disease-control efforts.**

2. New initiatives

66. Despite all we know about the human toll of HIV/AIDS - the numbers of infections, the deaths, the children who are orphaned - we are left to guess what the long-term effect of the pandemic will be on the States most afflicted by the disease. While HIV/AIDS depletes the capacity of States and economies in Africa faster than it can be replenished, we do not know the cumulative effects of loss of government officials, skilled health professionals, teachers, service providers, caregivers, police, soldiers and peacekeepers. In the absence of good research into these questions, we cannot begin to develop a strategy for countering the long-term effects of HIV/AIDS on governance and State stability.

67. **The Security Council, working closely with UNAIDS, should host a second special session on HIV/AIDS as a threat to international peace and security, to explore the future effects of HIV/AIDS on States and societies, generate research on the problem and identify critical steps towards a long-term strategy for diminishing the threat.**

68. The fight against HIV/AIDS, tuberculosis and malaria depends on capable, responsible States with functioning public health systems. The absence of health facilities is the primary factor spurring the proliferation of malaria. Funding gaps are preventing health-sector reforms in many heavily burdened countries, particularly those in South Asia and sub-Saharan Africa. Inconsistent or partial treatment, resulting from insufficient funding, has allowed new strains of tuberculosis to develop that are far more difficult to treat. Even when programme funding for HIV/AIDS is available, inadequate or non-existent health facilities in the poorest areas of sub-Saharan Africa hinder programmes from being effectively or sustainably implemented. **International donors, in partnership with national authorities and local civil society organizations, should undertake a major new global initiative to rebuild local and national public health systems throughout the developing world.**

69. Such efforts should be undertaken simultaneously with improving global disease monitoring capabilities. This is triply imperative - as a means of fighting new emerging infectious disease, defending against the threat of biological terrorism and building effective, responsible States. **Members of the World Health Assembly should provide greater resources to the WHO Global**

Outbreak Alert and Response Network to increase its capacity to cope with potential disease outbreaks.

70.   In extreme cases of threat posed by a new emerging infectious disease or intentional release of an infectious agent, there may be a need for cooperation between WHO and the Security Council in establishing effective quarantine measures (see section V below).

71.   In order to address problems of climate change modern economies need to reduce their dependence on hydrocarbons and should undertake a special effort to devise climate-friendly development strategies. Member States should place special attention on the development of low-carbon energy sources, including natural gas, renewable power and nuclear power, and should place special emphasis on the development of low-greenhouse-gas technologies. The Kyoto Protocol to the United Nations Framework Convention on Climate Change has encouraged the development of renewable energy sources that could gradually correct today's excessive dependency on fossil fuels. To further encourage this, **States should provide incentives for the further development of renewable energy sources and begin to phase out environmentally harmful subsidies, especially for fossil fuel use and development.**

72.   The entry into force of the Kyoto Protocol after ratification by the Russian Federation is a positive development, even though the Protocol by itself is not sufficient to solve the challenge of limiting greenhouse gas emissions. The Protocol has encouraged the development of renewable energy sources that could gradually correct today's excessive dependency on fossil fuels. Yet problems remain. Some advanced industrialized nations are on track to meet their Kyoto targets for reasons outside the realm of climate policy, e.g., a sharp reduction in their industrial production. The United States, which accounts for about one quarter of world emissions of greenhouse gases, refuses to ratify the Protocol. At the same time, developing countries, which now account for almost half of today's net emissions of greenhouse gases (but only one tenth of per capita emissions), have been opposed to accepting any binding emission caps, which they perceive to be impediments to economic growth. Industrialized nations are likely to be more resistant to accepting costly reductions without increased developing country participation. Most importantly, the Protocol does not contain any obligations beyond 2012. **We urge Member States to reflect on the gap between the promise of the Kyoto Protocol and its performance, re-engage on the problem of global warming and begin new negotiations to produce a new long-term strategy for reducing global warming beyond the period covered by the Protocol.**

73. The United Nations and the international financial institutions should also do more to assist those States most vulnerable to severe natural disasters, the effects of which can be destablizing as they were in 2004 in Haiti. The World Meteorological Association has estimated that investments in vulnerability reduction could drastically reduce the number of deaths associated with natural disasters. The United Nations Environment Programme (UNEP), the United Nations Development Programme (UNDP) and the World Bank should work in a more integrated fashion - and in partnership with Governments and outside research institutions - to improve vulnerability assessments and work with the most affected Governments to strengthen their adaptive capacity.

IV. Conflict between and within States

A. The threat of inter-State conflict

74. Although the world has seen few inter-State wars over the past 60 years, the threat of inter-State war has not vanished. Unresolved regional disputes in South Asia, North-East Asia and the Middle East continue to threaten international peace and security. These disputes may unravel 40 years of efforts to prevent the proliferation of nuclear weapons and more than 75 years of efforts to banish the scourge of biological and chemical weapons. In turn, inter-State rivalry in some regions fuels and exacerbates internal wars, making them more difficult to bring to a close. Such rivalry, by promoting conventional weapons build-ups, diverts scarce resources that could be used to reduce poverty, improve health and increase education.

75. War and ongoing instability in Iraq and Palestine have fuelled extremism in parts of the Muslim world and the West. This issue is complex and multidimensional and defies any simplistic categorization. Nonetheless, one cannot ignore the ability of extremist groups to foster perceptions within the West and within the Muslim world of cultural and religious antagonism between them, the dangers of which, if left unchecked, are profound.

76. In the past, the United Nations helped to reduce the threat of inter-State conflicts through the Secretary-General's "good offices", or quiet diplomacy aimed at defusing crises and providing hostile parties the opportunity to talk freely and test intentions. Successive Secretaries-General have played this role despite little capacity within the Organization to support it.

77. With the end of the cold war, the Security Council became increasingly active in addressing international threats. The average annual number of resolutions it passed increased from 15 to 60, or from one resolution a month to one a week. Before 1989, the Council applied sanctions twice; since then it has imposed

sanctions 14 times and for an increasingly diverse range of stated purposes, including to reverse aggression, restore democratic Governments, protect human rights, end wars, combat terrorism and support peace agreements.

78. Several of these sanctions regimes were at least partially effective. In some cases, they helped to produce negotiated agreements. In others, they combined with military pressure to weaken and isolate rebel groups and States in flagrant violation of Security Council resolutions.

79. Sanctions failed when they were not effectively targeted and when the Security Council failed to enforce them. Weak enforcement results from the strategic interests of powerful States; a lack of clarity about the purpose of sanctions; "sanctions fatigue" brought about by concern over their humanitarian impact; insufficient support from the respective sanctions committees; and insufficient State capacity to implement sanctions.

> *Sanctions failed when they were not effectively targeted and when the Security Council failed to enforce them.*

80. As a result of growing concern over the humanitarian impact of comprehensive sanctions, the Security Council stopped imposing them after the cases of Iraq, former Yugoslavia and Haiti, and turned exclusively to the use of financial, diplomatic, arms, aviation, travel and commodity sanctions, targeting the belligerents and policy makers most directly responsible for reprehensible policies.

81. Increased activity does not necessarily produce increased results. Not all situations that justified Security Council attention received it and not all its resolutions were followed by effective enforcement action. Yet two trends of the 1990s indicate increasing effectiveness in regulating international conflict. First, with the Council increasingly active and willing to use its powers under Chapter VII of the Charter of the United Nations, the balance between unilateral use of force and collectively authorized force has shifted dramatically. Collectively authorized use of force may not be the rule today, but it is no longer an exception. Second, and perhaps the most striking indicator of the growing importance of the role of the United Nations in regulating international conflict, is the recent expectation that the Security Council should be the arbiter of the use of force.

82. Many people assumed it was quite natural that the United States should seek Security Council support for going to war against Iraq in 2003. Superpowers, however, have rarely sought Security Council approval for their actions. That all States should seek Security Council authorization to use force is not a time-honoured principle; if this were the case, our faith in it would be much stronger. Our analysis suggests quite the opposite - that what is at stake is a relatively new emerging norm, one that is precious but not yet deep-rooted.

83. The case of Iraq prompted much difference of opinion. Some contend that the Security Council was ineffective because it could not produce Iraqi compliance

with its resolutions. Others argue Security Council irrelevance because the Council did not deter the United States and its coalition partners from waging war. Still others suggest that the refusal of the Security Council to bow to United States pressure to legitimate the war is proof of its relevance and indispensability: although the Security Council did not deter war, it provided a clear and principled standard with which to assess the decision to go to war. The flood of Foreign Ministers into the Security Council chambers during the debates, and widespread public attention, suggest that the United States decision to bring the question of force to the Security Council reaffirmed not just the relevance but the centrality of the Charter of the United Nations.

B. The threat of internal conflict

In the last 15 years, more civil wars were ended through negotiation than in the previous two centuries in large part because the United Nations provided leadership, opportunities for negotiation, strategic co-ordination, and the resources needed for implementation.

84. Since the end of the cold war, peacemaking, peace-keeping and post-conflict peacebuilding in civil wars have become the operational face of the United Nations in international peace and security.

85. The rapid growth of United Nations activity in civil wars coincides with a sharp decline in their numbers (see figure below). Since 1992, civil wars have declined steadily, and by 2003 had dropped by roughly 40 per cent to less than 30 wars. In the last

Ending civil wars and building peace
1970-2002

Source: Department of Peace and Conflict Research at Uppsala University; and International Peace Research Institute, Oslo.

15 years, more civil wars were ended through negotiation than in the previous two centuries in large part because the United Nations provided leadership, opportunities for negotiation, strategic coordination, and the resources needed for implementation. Hundreds of thousands of lives were saved, and regional and international stability were enhanced.

86.   This unprecedented success, however, was also coupled with major failures. Mediation produced settlement in only about 25 per cent of civil wars and only some of those attracted the political and material resources necessary for successful implementation. As a result, many implementation efforts failed, sometimes with disastrous consequences. If two peace agreements, the 1991 Bicesse Agreement for Angola and the 1993 Arusha Accords for Rwanda, had been successfully implemented, deaths attributable to war in the 1990s would have been reduced by several million. If the Security Council had been seriously committed to consolidating peace in Afghanistan in the early 1990s, more lives could have been saved, the Taliban might never have come to power and Al-Qaida could have been deprived of its most important sanctuary.

If the 1991 Bicesse Agreement for Angola and the 1993 Arusha Accords for Rwanda, had been successfully implemented, deaths attributable to war in the 1990s would have been reduced by several million.

87.   The biggest failures of the United Nations in civil violence have been in halting ethnic cleansing and genocide. In Rwanda, Secretariat officials failed to provide the Security Council with early warning of extremist plans to kill thousands of Tutsis and moderate Hutus. When the genocide started, troop contributors withdrew peacekeepers, and the Security Council, bowing to United States pressure, failed to respond. In Bosnia and Herzegovina, United Nations peacekeeping and the protection of humanitarian aid became a substitute for political and military action to stop ethnic cleansing and genocide. In Kosovo, paralysis in the Security Council led the North Atlantic Treaty Organization (NATO) to bypass the United Nations. Only in one instance in the 1990s - in East Timor - did the Security Council, urged on by the Secretary-General, work together with national Governments and regional actors to apply concerted pressure swiftly to halt large-scale killing.

88.   The large loss of life in such wars and outbreaks of mass violence obliges the international community to be more vigilant in preventing them. When prevention fails, there is urgent need to stop the killing and prevent any further return to war.

C. Meeting the challenge of prevention

1. Better international regulatory frameworks and norms

89.   The role of the United Nations in preventing wars can be strengthened by giv-
      ing more attention to developing international regimes and norms to govern
      some of the sources and accelerators of conflict. A very wide range of laws,
      norms, agreements and arrangements are relevant here, covering legal regimes
      and dispute resolution mechanisms, arms control and disarmament regimes,
      and dialogue and cooperation arrangements. Some examples are set out below.

90.   In the area of legal mechanisms, there have been few more important recent
      developments than the Rome Statute creating the International Criminal
      Court. In cases of mounting conflict, early indication by the Security Council
      that it is carefully monitoring the conflict in question and that it is willing to
      use its powers under the Rome Statute might deter parties from committing
      crimes against humanity and violating the laws of war. **The Security Council
      should stand ready to use the authority it has under the Rome Statute to
      refer cases to the International Criminal Court.**

91.   More legal mechanisms are necessary in the area of natural resources, fights
      over which have often been an obstacle to peace. Alarmed by the inflamma-
      tory role of natural resources in wars in Sierra Leone, Angola and the
      Democratic Republic of the Congo, civil society organizations and the
      Security Council have turned to the "naming and shaming" of, and the
      imposition of sanctions against, individuals and corporations involved in
      illicit trade, and States have made a particular attempt to restrict the sale of
      "conflict diamonds". Evidence from Sierra Leone and Angola suggests that
      such efforts contributed to ending those civil wars. A new challenge for the
      United Nations is to provide support to weak States - especially, but not lim-
      ited to, those recovering from war - in the management of their natural
      resources to avoid future conflicts.

92.   **The United Nations should work with national authorities, interna-
      tional financial institutions, civil society organizations and the private
      sector to develop norms governing the management of natural
      resources for countries emerging from or at risk of conflict.**

93.   There should also be a focus on the development of rules, for example through
      the International Law Commission, for the use of transboundary resources, such
      as water, oil and gas.

94.   The United Nations should seek to work closely with regional organizations
      that have taken the lead in building frameworks for prevention. The United
      Nations can benefit from sharing information and analysis with regional

early-warning systems, but more importantly regional organizations have gone farther than the United Nations in setting normative standards that can guide preventive efforts. For example, the Organization of American States (OAS) and the African Union (AU) agree on the need to protect elected Governments from coups. The Organization of Security and Cooperation in Europe (OSCE) has developed operational norms on minority rights. **The United Nations should build on the experience of regional organizations in developing frameworks for minority rights and the protection of democratically elected Governments from unconstitutional overthrow.**

95. In the area of arms control and disarmament regimes, much more needs to be done, not only in the context of nuclear, biological and chemical weapons (see section V below) but in relation to the proliferation of small arms and light weapons. In the 1990s, small arms, light weapons and landmines were the primary weapons in most civil wars. While concerted action by civil society organizations and concerned Member States led to a ban on landmines, efforts to limit the widespread availability of small arms and light weapons have barely moved beyond rhetoric to action.

96. A comprehensive approach to the small arms problem emerged in the late 1990s and seeks to create international action to limit their production and spread. The key global instrument for this approach is the United Nations Programme of Action to Prevent, Combat and Eradicate the Illicit Trade in Small Arms and Light Weapons in All Its Aspects, a comprehensive set of recommendations aimed at preventing and eradicating the illicit manufacture, transfer and circulation of small arms and light weapons. The Programme of Action makes innovative use of regional bodies, such as the Nairobi Secretariat, which, *inter alia,* monitors the implementation of the Nairobi Protocol for the Prevention, Control and Reduction of Small Arms and Light Weapons in the Great Lakes Region and the Horn of Africa, to report, monitor and verify State compliance. It should be considered a start rather than an end-point for United Nations efforts. **Member States should expedite and conclude negotiations on legally binding agreements on the marking and tracing, as well as the brokering and transfer, of small arms and light weapons.**

97. The United Nations can also help to prevent inter-State conflict by increasing the transparency of Member States' conventional weapons holdings and acquisitions. The United Nations Register of Conventional Arms, established in 1991, enhances military transparency by soliciting annual declarations of Member States on their sale and purchase of conventional weapons and existing weapons holdings, as well as their defence postures, policies and doctrines. However, the Register is marred by incomplete, untimely and inaccurate

reporting. **All Member States should report completely and accurately on all elements of the United Nations Register of Conventional Arms, and the Secretary-General should be asked to report annually to the General Assembly and Security Council on any inadequacies in the reporting.**

2. Better information and analysis

98. Prevention requires early warning and analysis that is based on objective and impartial research. Although the United Nations has some early-warning and analysis capacity scattered among different agencies and departments, the Secretary-General has not been able to establish any properly-resourced unit able to integrate inputs from these offices into early-warning reports and strategy options for purposes of decision-making. The best option for creating a coherent capacity for developing strategic options is to strengthen the Office of the Secretary-General through the creation of a Deputy Secretary-General for Peace and Security (see section XIX below).

99. Although some field-based agencies participate in early-warning mechanisms and international non-governmental organizations have played a major role in recent years in providing timely information, analysis and advocacy, the Secretary-General's access to local analysis of conflict is sharply limited. Greater interaction by United Nations political, peacekeeping and humanitarian departments with outside sources of early-warning information and of local knowledge of conflicts would enhance United Nations conflict management. Also, in the past few years, research institutions (in academia and in other international organizations) have begun to compile both the necessary data and sophisticated analysis of various causes and accelerators of different kinds of conflict. United Nations policy sections should engage more actively with local sources of knowledge and outside sources of research.

3. Preventive diplomacy and mediation

100. United Nations efforts to prevent outbreaks of internal violence have met with less success than its efforts to prevent inter-State wars, and they are often inhibited by the reluctance of Member States to see their domestic affairs internationalized. But more effort could and should be made in this area, particularly through the appointment of skilled, experienced and regionally knowledgeable envoys, mediators and special representatives, who can make as important a contribution to conflict prevention as they do to conflict resolution.

101. In making such appointments, the Secretary-General should place high-level competence above all other criteria and do more to nurture internal and exter-

nal expertise in this respect. **This would be made easier by the establishment of a facility for training and briefing new or potential special representatives and other United Nations mediators, and we so recommend.**

102. Mediators and negotiators need adequate support. Although the demand for United Nations mediation has skyrocketed in the past 10 years, resources devoted to this function have remained minimal. The deliberate underresourcing of the Department of Political Affairs of the United Nations Secretariat by Member States is at odds with these same States' professed desire for a strong United Nations. **The Department of Political Affairs should be given additional resources and should be restructured to provide more consistent and professional mediation support.**

103. While the details of such a restructuring should be left to the Secretary-General, it should take into account the need for the United Nations to have:

     (a) A field-oriented, dedicated mediation support capacity, comprised of a small team of professionals with relevant direct experience and expertise, available to all United Nations mediators;

     (b) Competence on thematic issues that recur in peace negotiations, such as the sequencing of implementation steps, the design of monitoring arrangements, the sequencing of transitional arrangements and the design of national reconciliation mechanisms;

     (c) Greater interaction with national mediators, regional organizations and non-governmental organizations involved in conflict resolution;

     (d) Greater consultation with and involvement in peace processes of important voices from civil society, especially those of women, who are often neglected during negotiations.

4. Preventive deployment

104. In cases of mounting tensions, the early deployment of peacekeepers can reassure parties seeking peaceful resolution to a conflict and deter would-be aggressors. It is notable that the only clear case of preventive deployment to date, in the former Yugoslav Republic of Macedonia, was requested by the national authorities and was manifestly a success. **We encourage national leaders and parties to conflict to make constructive use of the option of preventive deployment.**

105. The Security Council should also note that in countries that have emerged from conflict, the deployment of small numbers of peacekeepers to train national armed forces can serve an important preventive function.

106. Good communication between mediators and peacekeeping planners can also help identify opportunities for preventive deployments. The now occasional practice of peacekeeping planners sitting in on mediation processes should be standardized.

V. Nuclear, radiological, chemical and biological weapons

A. The threats we face

1. Nuclear weapons

107. Any use of nuclear weapons, by accident or design, risks human casualties and economic dislocation on a catastrophic scale. Stopping the proliferation of such weapons - and their potential use, by either State or non-State actors - must remain an urgent priority for collective security.

108. The threat posed by nuclear proliferation - the spread of nuclear weapons among States - arises in two ways. The first and most immediate concern is that some countries, under cover of their current Treaty on the Non-Proliferation of Nuclear Weapons membership, will covertly and illegally develop full-scale weapons programmes, or that - acting within the letter but perhaps not the spirit of the Treaty - they will acquire all the materials and expertise needed for weapons programmes with the option of withdrawing from the Treaty at the point when they are ready to proceed with weaponization.

109. The second longer-term, concern is about the erosion and possible collapse of the whole Treaty regime. Almost 60 States currently operate or are construct- ing nuclear power or research reactors, and at least 40 possess the industrial and scientific infrastructure which would enable them, if they chose, to build nuclear weapons at relatively short notice if the legal and normative constraints of the Treaty regime no longer apply.

110. Both concerns are now very real: the Treaty on the Non-Proliferation of Nuclear Weapons is not as effective a constraint as it was. In 1963, when only four States had nuclear arsenals, the United States Government predicted that the following decade would see the emergence of 15 to 25 nuclear-weapon States; others predicted the number would be as high as 50. As of 2004, only eight States are known to have nuclear arsenals. The strong non-proliferation regime - embodied in IAEA and the Treaty itself - helped dramatically to slow the predicted rate of proliferation. It made three critical contributions: it bolstered a normative prohibition against the ownership, use and prolifer- ation of these weapons; it ensured that States could benefit from nuclear technologies, but with oversight; and it reassured States about the capacities

of neighbours and potential rivals, allowing them to avoid unnecessary arms races.

111.   But the nuclear non-proliferation regime is now at risk because of lack of compliance with existing commitments, withdrawal or threats of withdrawal from the Treaty on the Non-Proliferation of Nuclear Weapons to escape those commitments, a changing international security environment and the diffusion of technology. We are approaching a point at which the erosion of the non-proliferation regime could become irreversible and result in a cascade of proliferation.

112.   Regardless of whether more States acquire nuclear weapons, there are also grave risks posed by the existence of large stockpiles of nuclear and radiological materials. Today 1,300 kilograms of highly enriched uranium exist in research reactors in 27 countries. The total volume of HEU stockpiles is far greater, and many HEU storage sites in the world are inadequately secured. States have publicly confirmed 20 cases of nuclear material diversion and more than 200 incidents involving illicit trafficking in nuclear materials have been documented over the past decade. Scientists have repeatedly warned of the ease with which terrorists could, with parts from the open market, assemble a simple "gun-type" nuclear device that simply collides two quantities of HEU. Experts suggest that if a simple nuclear device were detonated in a major city, the number of deaths would range from tens of thousands to more than one million. The shock to international commerce, employment and travel would amount to at least one trillion dollars. Such an attack could have further, far-reaching implications for international security, democratic governance and civil rights.

... the nuclear non-proliferation regime is now at risk ...

2. Radiological weapons

113.   A different threat is posed by radiological weapons, which are more weapons of mass disruption than mass destruction. Radiological weapons can use plutonium or highly enriched uranium but can rely simply on radioactive materials, of which there are millions of sources used in medical and industrial facilities worldwide. The immediate destructive effect of a radiological or "dirty" bomb is only as great as its conventional explosive, and even the radiation effects of such a bomb are likely to be limited. The more harmful effects of disruption and economic damage would be prompted by public alarm and the necessity of evacuating and decontaminating affected areas. The ubiquity of radiological materials and the crude requirements for detonating such a device suggest a high likelihood of use. This puts a premium on educating the public about the limited consequences of radiological weapons in order to mitigate some of the alarm and uncertainty that would be unleashed in the event of an attack.

3. Chemical and biological weapons

114. Chemical and biological materials also pose a growing threat: they share with nuclear weapons the awful potential of being used in a single attack to inflict mass casualties. Chemical agents are widespread and relatively easy to acquire and weaponize. There are almost 6,000 industrial chemical facilities worldwide, posing potential targets and opportunities for the acquisition of materials. Chemical-weapon States have lagged behind in the destruction of chemical weapons scheduled by the Chemical Weapons Convention: of the 70,000 metric tons of declared weapons agents, the Organization for the Prohibition of Chemical Weapons (OPCW) has verified the destruction of only 9,600, and if the current pace persists, the Convention's goal of the complete destruction of chemical weapons agents will not be met even by the agreed extended deadline of 2012.

While scientific advances in the biotechnology sector hold out the prospect of prevention and cure for many diseases, they also increase opportunities for the development of deadly new ones.

115. While rapid growth and scientific advances in the biotechnology sector hold out the prospect of prevention and cure for many diseases, they also increase opportunities for the development of deadly new ones. Dramatic advances in recombinant DNA technology and direct genetic manipulation raise the spectre of "designer bugs", which may be developed to reconstruct eradicated diseases and to resist existing vaccinations, antibiotics and other treatments. There are countless fermentation, medical and research facilities equipped to produce biological agents. Meanwhile, the biological toxin ricin has been discovered in several terrorist workshops. Unlike anthrax, which can be treated by antibiotics, ricin has no antidote and is lethal to humans in quantities smaller than the size of a pinhead. Use of similar materials to cause deliberate outbreaks of infectious disease could prove equally if not more lethal than a nuclear detonation. Under worst-case assumptions, an attack using only one gram of weaponized smallpox could produce between 100,000 and 1,000,000 fatalities.

116. That a high-damage attack has not occurred is not a cause for complacency but a call for urgent prevention.

B. Meeting the challenge of prevention

117. Multilayered action is required. The first layer of an effective strategy to prevent the proliferation of nuclear, radiological, chemical and biological weapons should feature global instruments that reduce the demand for them. The second layer should contain global instruments that operate on the supply side - to limit the capacity of both States and non-State actors to acquire weapons and

the materials and expertise needed to build them. The third layer must consist of Security Council enforcement activity underpinned by credible, shared information and analysis. The fourth layer must comprise national and international civilian and public health defence.

1. Better strategies to reduce demand

118. Lacklustre disarmament by the nuclear-weapon States weakens the diplomatic force of the non-proliferation regime and thus its ability to constrain proliferation. Despite Security Council commitment to the contrary (resolution 984 (1995)), these nuclear-weapon States are increasingly unwilling to pledge assurances of non-use (negative security assurances) and they maintain the right to retaliate with nuclear weapons against chemical or biological attack.

119. Despite the end of the cold war, nuclear-weapon States earn only a mixed grade in fulfilling their disarmament commitments. While the United States and the Russian Federation have dismantled roughly half of their nuclear weapons, committed to large reductions in deployed strategic warheads and eliminated most of their non-strategic nuclear weapons, such progress has been overshadowed by recent reversals. In 2000, the nuclear-weapon States committed to 13 practical steps towards nuclear disarmament, which were all but renounced by them at the 2004 meeting of the Preparatory Committee for the 2005 Review Conference of the Parties to the Treaty on the Non-Proliferation of Nuclear Weapons.

120. **The nuclear-weapon States must take several steps to restart disarmament:**

    (a) **They must honour their commitments under article VI of the Treaty on the Non-Proliferation of Nuclear Weapons to move towards disarmament and be ready to undertake specific measures in fulfilment of those commitments;**

    (b) **They should reaffirm their previous commitments not to use nuclear weapons against non-nuclear-weapon States,** to further diminish the perceived value of nuclear weapons, and secure robust international cooperation to staunch proliferation, formalizing such commitments in pending and future nuclear-weapon-free zones agreements.

121. **The United States and the Russian Federation, other nuclear-weapon States and States not party to the Treaty on the Non-Proliferation of Nuclear Weapons should commit to practical measures to reduce the risk of accidental nuclear war, including, where appropriate, a progressive schedule for de-alerting their strategic nuclear weapons.**

122. In addition, we believe it would be valuable if the Security Council explicitly pledged to take collective action in response to a nuclear attack or the threat of such attack on a non-nuclear-weapon State.

123. Given the challenge to the nuclear non-proliferation regime posed by States not party to the Treaty on the Non-Proliferation of Nuclear Weapons, and recognizing the impact of that challenge on regional insecurity, we recommend that negotiations to resolve regional conflicts include confidence-building measures and steps towards disarmament.

124. States not party to the Treaty on the Non-Proliferation of Nuclear Weapons should pledge a commitment to non-proliferation and disarmament, demonstrating their commitment by ratifying the Comprehensive Nuclear-Test-Ban Treaty and supporting negotiations for a fissile material cut-off treaty, both of which are open to nuclear-weapon and non-nuclear-weapon States alike. We recommend that peace efforts in the Middle East and South Asia launch nuclear disarmament talks that could lead to the establishment of nuclear-weapon-free zones in those regions similar to those established for Latin America and the Caribbean, Africa, the South Pacific and South-East Asia.

125. For biological and chemical weapons, there is both an obligation and a historic opportunity to fully eliminate all declared chemical weapons stockpiles: all chemical-weapon States should expedite the scheduled destruction of all existing chemical weapons stockpiles by the agreed target date of 2012.

126. Verification of the Chemical Weapons Convention should also be further strengthened, and the long-standing impasse over a verification mechanism for the Biological and Toxin Weapons Convention, which has undermined confidence in the overall regime, should be overcome. States parties to the Biological and Toxin Weapons Convention should without delay return to negotiations for a credible verification protocol, inviting the active participation of the biotechnology industry. States parties to the Biological and Toxin Weapons Convention and the Chemical Weapons Convention must increase bilateral diplomatic pressure to universalize membership.

2. Better strategies to reduce supply

127. We recognize that nuclear energy, in the view of many, is an important source of power for civilian uses and may become even more crucial in the context of a worldwide effort to reduce dependency on fossil fuels and emissions of greenhouse gases. At the same time, the mounting tension between the goals of

achieving a more effective non-proliferation regime and the right of all signatories of the Treaty on the Non-Proliferation of Nuclear Weapons to develop civilian nuclear industries needs to be addressed and defused.

128. Article IV of the Treaty on the Non-Proliferation of Nuclear Weapons guarantees States parties' rights to develop the research, production and use of nuclear energy for peaceful purposes; this right must be preserved. The Treaty also specifies that this right must be used in conformity with its articles I and II; this obligation also must be respected. In recent years, it has become clear that the proliferation risks from the enrichment of uranium and from the reprocessing of spent fuel are great and increasing. These two processes in particular provide a route by which Treaty signatories can (and in some cases have) clandestinely pursued activities not in conformity with the Treaty and designed to give them the option of acquiring a nuclear-weapon capability.

129. Two remedies are required. First, the inspection and verification rules that have governed IAEA through the mid-1990s have proven increasingly inadequate. IAEA initiated more stringent inspection rules in the Model Additional Protocol, but as yet only one third of the States parties to the Treaty on the Non-Proliferation of Nuclear Weapons have ratified the Protocol. **The IAEA Board of Governors should recognize the Model Additional Protocol as today's standard for IAEA safeguards, and the Security Council should be prepared to act in cases of serious concern over non-compliance with non-proliferation and safeguards standards.**

130. Second, **we urge that negotiations be engaged without delay and carried forward to an early conclusion on an arrangement, based on the existing provisions of articles III and IX of the IAEA statute, which would enable IAEA to act as a guarantor for the supply of fissile material to civilian nuclear users.** Such an arrangement would need to put the Agency in a position to meet, through suppliers it authorized, demands for nuclear fuel supplies of low enriched uranium and for the reprocessing of spent fuel at market rates and to provide a guarantee of uninterrupted supply of these services, as long as there was no breach of safeguard or inspection procedures at the facilities in question.

131. **While that arrangement is being negotiated, States should, without surrendering the right under the Treaty on the Non-Proliferation of Nuclear Weapons to construct such facilities, voluntarily institute a time-limited moratorium on the construction of any further enrichment or reprocessing facilities, with a commitment to the moratorium matched by a guarantee of the supply of fissile materials by the current suppliers at market rates.**

132. Recent experience of the activities of the A.Q. Khan network has demonstrated the need for and the value of measures taken to interdict the illicit and clandestine trade in components for nuclear programmes. This problem is currently being addressed on a voluntary basis by the Proliferation Security Initiative. **We believe that all States should be encouraged to join this voluntary initiative.**

133. In order to reinforce international legal provisions against the illicit trafficking of nuclear, biological and chemical weapons and materials, ongoing negotiations at the International Maritime Organization (IMO) to amend the 1988 Convention for the Suppression of Unlawful Acts against the Safety of Maritime Navigation should be completed in a timely manner. The Security Council may need to be prepared to consider mandatory action if progress in the Convention negotiations is unsatisfactory.

134. While the Treaty on the Non-Proliferation of Nuclear Weapons provides the right of withdrawal from the Treaty, States should be urged not to do so. Those who withdraw should be held responsible for violations committed while still a party to the Treaty. **A State's notice of withdrawal from the Treaty on the Non-Proliferation of Nuclear Weapons should prompt immediate verification of its compliance with the Treaty, if necessary mandated by the Security Council. The IAEA Board of Governors should resolve that, in the event of violations, all assistance provided by IAEA should be withdrawn.**

135. Urgent short-term action is needed to defend against the possible terrorist use of nuclear, radiological, chemical and biological weapons. High priority must be accorded to consolidating, securing, and when possible eliminating potentially hazardous materials, and implementing effective export controls. To that end, we welcome the Global Threat Reduction Initiative, which facilitates (a) the reduction of global highly enriched uranium stockpiles, (b) the conversion of HEU research reactors to "proliferation-resistant" reactors, and (c) the "downblending" of existing HEU. **The proposed timeline for implementing the Global Threat Reduction Initiative should be halved from 10 to 5 years.**

136. The Security Council, acting under its resolution 1540 (2004), can offer States model legislation for security, tracking, criminalization and export controls, and by 2006 develop minimum standards for United Nations Member State implementation. To achieve that goal, the implementation committee of Council resolution 1540 (2004) should establish a permanent liaison with IAEA, OPCW and the Nuclear Suppliers Group.

137. **States parties to the Biological and Toxin Weapons Convention should also negotiate a new bio-security protocol to classify dangerous biological agents and establish binding international standards for the export of**

such agents. Within a designated time frame, States parties to the Convention should refrain from participating in such biotechnology commerce with non-members.

138. IAEA member States should increase funding for its programmes that help to locate and secure radioactive sources and that assist States in establishing pertinent domestic legislation. **Moreover, the Conference on Disarmament should move without further delay to negotiate a verifiable fissile material cut-off treaty that, on a designated schedule, ends the production of highly enriched uranium for non-weapon as well as weapons purposes.**

3. Better enforcement capability

139. The Security Council today has few arrows in its quiver other than sanctions and military force to enforce non-proliferation agreements. Moreover, a special referral to the Security Council that results in no action is worse than no referral. The ability of the Security Council to generate credible information about potential instances of proliferation should be strengthened.

140. To that end, links between IAEA and OPCW and the Security Council must also be strengthened. **The Directors-General of IAEA and OPCW should be invited by the Security Council to report to it twice-yearly on the status of safeguards and verification processes, as well as on any serious concerns they have which might fall short of an actual breach of the Treaty on the Non-Proliferation of Nuclear Weapons and the Chemical Weapons Convention.**

141. The Security Council should also be prepared to deploy inspection capacities for suspected nuclear and chemical violations, drawing on the capacities of IAEA and OPCW. Until multilateral negotiations yield a Biological and Toxin Weapons Convention verification mechanism, the Security Council should avail itself of the Secretary-General's roster of inspectors for biological weapons, who should remain independent and work under United Nations staff codes. This roster of inspectors should also be available to advise the Council and liaise with WHO authorities in the event of a suspicious disease outbreak, as discussed below.

4. Better public health defences

142. Scientific advancements in biotechnology and the ubiquity of facilities capable of producing biological agents circumscribe prospects for the elimination of biological weapons and complicate verification efforts. But unlike nuclear weapons, many (though not all) biological agents can be countered by vaccinations and effective responses (including rapid diagnosis, quarantines and treat-

ment). Well-prepared societies may thus be able to avoid the worst-case scenarios of biological attacks.

143. However, at present, international aid for infectious disease monitoring, detection and response is lacking, security planning and spending are poorly coordinated with health-care policies and budgets, and there is insufficient understanding that an inevitable, new biological future makes active bio-defence the most viable option against the likelihood of attack.

144. Given the potential international security threat posed by the intentional release of an infectious biological agent or an overwhelming natural outbreak of an infectious disease, there is a need for the WHO Director-General, through the Secretary-General, to keep the Security Council informed during any suspicious or overwhelming outbreak of infectious disease. In such an event, the Security Council should be prepared to support the work of WHO investigators or to deploy experts reporting directly to the Council, and if existing International Health Regulations do not provide adequate access for WHO investigations and response coordination, the Security Council should be prepared to mandate greater compliance. In the event that a State is unable to adequately quarantine large numbers of potential carriers, the Security Council should be prepared to support international action to assist in cordon operations. **The Security Council should consult with the WHO Director-General to establish the necessary procedures for working together in the event of a suspicious or overwhelming outbreak of infectious disease.**

VI. Terrorism

A. The threat we face

145. Terrorism attacks the values that lie at the heart of the Charter of the United Nations: respect for human rights; the rule of law; rules of war that protect civilians; tolerance among peoples and nations; and the peaceful resolution of conflict. Terrorism flourishes in environments of despair, humiliation, poverty, political oppression, extremism and human rights abuse; it also flourishes in contexts of regional conflict and foreign occupation; and it profits from weak State capacity to maintain law and order.

146. Two new dynamics give the terrorist threat greater urgency. Al-Qaida is the first instance - not likely to be the last - of an armed non-State network with global reach and sophisticated capacity. Attacks against more than 10 Member States on four continents in the past five years have demonstrated that Al-Qaida and associated entities pose a universal threat to the membership of the United Nations and the United Nations itself. In public statements, Al-Qaida has sin-

gled out the United Nations as a major obstacle to its goals and defined it as one of its enemies. Second, the threat that terrorists - of whatever type, with whatever motivation - will seek to cause mass casualties creates unprecedented dangers. Our recommendations provided above on controlling the supply of nuclear, radiological, chemical and biological materials and building robust global public health systems are central to a strategy to prevent this threat.

B. Meeting the challenge of prevention

1. A comprehensive strategy

147. Throughout the Panel's regional consultations, it heard concerns from Governments and civil society organizations that the current "war on terrorism" has in some instances corroded the very values that terrorists target: human rights and the rule of law. Most of those who expressed such concerns did not question the seriousness of the terrorist threat and acknowledged that the right to life is the most fundamental of human rights. They did, however, express fears that approaches to terror focusing wholly on military, police and intelligence measures risk undermining efforts to promote good governance and human rights, alienate large parts of the world's population and thereby weaken the potential for collective action against terrorism. The crucial need, in relation to the States in the regions from which terrorists originate, is to address not only their capacity but their will to fight terror. To develop that will - with States drawing support rather than opposition from their own publics - requires a broader-based approach.

Terrorism attacks the values that lie at the heart of the Charter of the United Nations: respect for human rights; the rule of law; rules of war that protect civilians; tolerance among peoples and nations; and the peaceful resolution of conflict.

148. A thread that runs through all such concerns is the imperative to develop a global strategy of fighting terrorism that addresses root causes and strengthens responsible States and the rule of law and fundamental human rights. What is required is a comprehensive strategy that incorporates but is broader than coercive measures. **The United Nations, with the Secretary-General taking a leading role, should promote such a comprehensive strategy, which includes:**

(a) **Dissuasion, working to reverse the causes or facilitators of terrorism, including through promoting social and political rights, the rule of law and democratic reform; working to end occupations and address major political grievances; combating organized crime; reducing poverty and unemployment; and stopping State collapse.** All of the strategies discussed above for preventing other threats have secondary benefits in working to remove some of the causes or facilitators of terrorism;

(b) **Efforts to counter extremism and intolerance, including through education and fostering public debate.** One recent innovation by UNDP, the *Arab Human Development Report*, has helped catalyse a wide ranging debate within the Middle East on the need for gender empowerment, political freedom, rule of law and civil liberties;

(c) **Development of better instruments for global counter-terrorism cooperation, all within a legal framework that is respectful of civil liberties and human rights, including in the areas of law enforcement; intelligence-sharing, where possible; denial and interdiction, when required; and financial controls;**

(d) **Building State capacity to prevent terrorist recruitment and operations;**

(e) **Control of dangerous materials and public health defence.**

2. Better counter-terrorism instruments

149. Several United Nations anti-terrorist conventions have laid important normative foundations. However, far too many States remain outside the conventions and not all countries ratifying the conventions proceed to adopt internal enforcement measures. Also, attempts to address the problem of terrorist financing have been inadequate. While in the three months after 11 September 2001 $112 million in alleged terrorist funds were frozen, only $24 million were frozen in the two years that followed. Seized funds represent only a small fraction of total funds available to terrorist organizations. While many States have insufficient anti-money-laundering laws and technical capacity, the evasion techniques of terrorists are highly developed and many terrorist funds have a legal origin and are hard to regulate.

150. **Member States that have not yet done so should actively consider signing and ratifying all 12 international conventions against terrorism, and should adopt the eight Special Recommendations on Terrorist Financing issued by the Organization for Economic Cooperation and Development (OECD)-supported Financial Action Task Force on Money-Laundering and the measures recommended in its various best practices papers.**

151. The Security Council has played an important role in filling gaps in counter-terrorism strategy. Since the early 1990s, the Security Council has attempted to weaken State support for and strengthen State resistance to terrorism. From 1992 onwards, the Security Council applied sanctions against individuals and States that supported terrorism - including, in 1999 and 2000, Osama Bin Laden and Al-Qaida and the Taliban. The initial response by the Security Council to the terrorist attacks of 11 September 2001 was swift and impressive. Security Council reso-

lution 1373 (2001) imposed uniform, mandatory counter-terrorist obligations on all States and established a Counter-Terrorism Committee to monitor compliance and to facilitate the provision of technical assistance to States.

152. However, the Security Council must proceed with caution. The way entities or individuals are added to the terrorist list maintained by the Council and the absence of review or appeal for those listed raise serious accountability issues and possibly violate fundamental human rights norms and conventions. **The Al-Qaida and Taliban Sanctions Committee should institute a process for reviewing the cases of individuals and institutions claiming to have been wrongly placed or retained on its watch lists.**

153. Sanctions imposed by the Security Council and the work of its Counter-Terrorism Committee have played an important role in ending the support of some States for terrorism and mobilizing other States in the fight against it. However, Council sanctions against Al-Qaida and Taliban suffer from lagging support and implementation by Member States and affect only a small subset of known Al-Qaida operatives, while a number of States are lagging behind in their compliance with the directives of the Counter-Terrorism Committee. We believe that further action is needed to achieve full implementation of these directives.

3. Assisting States in confronting terrorism

154. Because United Nations-facilitated assistance is limited to technical support, States seeking operational support for counter-terrorism activities have no alternative but to seek bilateral assistance. A United Nations capacity to facilitate this assistance would in some instances ease domestic political constraints, and this can be achieved by providing for the Counter-Terrorism Executive Directorate to act as a clearing house for State-to-State provision of military, police and border control assistance for the development of domestic counter-terrorism capacities. **The Security Council, after consultation with affected States, should extend the authority of the Counter-Terrorism Executive Directorate to perform this function.**

155. Non-compliance can be a matter of insufficient will but is more frequently a function of lack of capacity. United Nations members and specialized bodies should increase their efforts to provide States with access to effective legal, administrative and police tools to prevent terrorism. **To aid this process, the United Nations should establish a capacity-building trust fund under the Counter-Terrorism Executive Directorate.**

156. If confronted by States that have the capacity to undertake their obligations but repeatedly fail to do so, **the Security Council** may need to take additional

measures to ensure compliance, and **should devise a schedule of predeter-mined sanctions for State non-compliance.**

4. Defining terrorism

157. The United Nations ability to develop a comprehensive strategy has been con-strained by the inability of Member States to agree on an anti-terrorism conven-tion including a definition of terrorism. This prevents the United Nations from exerting its moral authority and from sending an unequivocal message that ter-rorism is never an acceptable tactic, even for the most defensible of causes.

158. Since 1945, an ever stronger set of norms and laws - including the Charter of the United Nations, the Geneva Conventions and the Rome Statute for the International Criminal Court - has regulated and constrained States' decisions to use force and their conduct in war - for example in the requirement to dis-tinguish between combatants and civilians, to use force proportionally and to live up to basic humanitarian principles. Violations of these obligations should continue to be met with widespread condemnation and war crimes should be prosecuted.

159. The norms governing the use of force by non-State actors have not kept pace with those pertaining to States. This is not so much a legal question as a politi-cal one. Legally, virtually all forms of terrorism are prohibited by one of 12 inter-national counter-terrorism conventions, international customary law, the Geneva Conventions or the Rome Statutes. Legal scholars know this, but there is a clear difference between this scattered list of conventions and little-known provisions of other treaties, and a compelling normative framework, understood by all, that should surround the question of terrorism. The United Nations must achieve the same degree of normative strength concerning non-State use of force as it has concerning State use of force. Lack of agreement on a clear and well-known definition undermines the normative and moral stance against terrorism and has stained the United Nations image. Achieving a comprehensive conven-tion on terrorism, including a clear definition, is a political imperative.

160. The search for an agreed definition usually stumbles on two issues. The first is the argument that any definition should include States' use of armed forces against civilians. We believe that the legal and normative framework against State violations is far stronger than in the case of non-State actors and we do not find this objection to be compelling. The second objection is that peoples under foreign occupation have a right to resistance and a definition of terrorism should not override this right. The right to resistance is contested by some. But it is not the central point: the central point is that there is nothing in the fact of occupation that justifies the targeting and killing of civilians.

161. Neither of these objections is weighty enough to contradict the argument that the strong, clear normative framework of the United Nations surrounding State use of force must be complemented by a normative framework of equal authority surrounding non-State use of force. Attacks that specifically target innocent civilians and non-combatants must be condemned clearly and unequivocally by all.

162. We welcome the recent passage of Security Council resolution 1566 (2004), which includes several measures to strengthen the role of the United Nations in combating terrorism.

163. Nevertheless, we believe there is particular value in achieving a consensus definition within the General Assembly, given its unique legitimacy in normative terms, and that it should rapidly complete negotiations on a comprehensive convention on terrorism.

164. That definition of terrorism should include the following elements:

   (a) recognition, in the preamble, that State use of force against civilians is regulated by the Geneva Conventions and other instruments, and, if of sufficient scale, constitutes a war crime by the persons concerned or a crime against humanity;

   (b) restatement that acts under the 12 preceding anti-terrorism conventions are terrorism, and a declaration that they are a crime under international law; and restatement that terrorism in time of armed conflict is prohibited by the Geneva Conventions and Protocols;

   (c) reference to the definitions contained in the 1999 International Convention for the Suppression of the Financing of Terrorism and Security Council resolution 1566 (2004);

   (d) description of terrorism as "any action, in addition to actions already specified by the existing conventions on aspects of terrorism, the Geneva Conventions and Security Council resolution 1566 (2004), that is intended to cause death or serious bodily harm to civilians or non-combatants, when the purpose of such act, by its nature or context, is to intimidate a population, or to compel a Government or an international organization to do or to abstain from doing any act".

VII. Transnational organized crime

A. The threat we face

165. Transnational organized crime is a menace to States and societies, eroding human security and the fundamental obligation of States to provide for law and order. Combating organized crime serves the double purpose of reducing this

direct threat to State and human security, and also constitutes a necessary step in the effort to prevent and resolve internal conflicts, combat the spread of weapons and prevent terrorism.

166. One of the core activities of organized criminal groups - drug trafficking - has major security implications. It is estimated that criminal organizations gain $300 to $500 billion annually from narcotics trafficking, their single largest source of income. In some regions, the huge profits generated through this activity even rivals some countries' GDP, thus threatening State authority, economic development and the rule of law. Drug trafficking has fuelled an increase in intravenous heroin use, which has contributed in some parts of the world to an alarming spread of the HIV/AIDS virus. There is growing evidence of a nexus between terrorist groups' financing and opium profits, most visibly in Afghanistan.

167. States and international organizations have reacted too slowly to the threat of organized crime and corruption. Statements about the seriousness of the threat have rarely been matched by action. Three basic impediments stand in the way of more effective international responses: insufficient cooperation among States, weak coordination among international agencies and inadequate compliance by many States.

168. Effectiveness in tackling specific incarnations of organized crime varies. Anticorruption efforts suffer from a lack of commitment and understanding about the types, levels, location and cost of corruption. In the effort to curb the supply of narcotics, successes in some countries are often offset by failures in others. National demand-reduction initiatives in the industrialized world have been similarly ineffective, and the total number of opium and heroin users has remained relatively stable over the last decade.

169. Responses to organized crime during and after conflict have been decentralized and fragmented. In the post-war period, former belligerents seek to exploit criminal connections and know-how developed during the war, thus undermining international peacebuilding efforts. Entrenched corruption, the use of violence to protect criminal activities and close ties between criminal enterprises and political elites hinder establishing the rule of law and effective State institutions. International efforts in curbing arms trafficking have been insufficient and sanctions regimes are insufficiently enforced.

170. Organized crime is increasingly operating through fluid networks rather than more formal hierarchies. This form of organization provides criminals with diversity, flexibility, low visibility and longevity. Connections among different networks became a major feature of the organized crime world during the 1990s, thus creating networks of networks. The agility of such networks stands in marked contrast to the cumbersome sharing of information and weak cooperation in criminal investigations and prosecutions on the part of States.

B. Meeting the challenge of prevention

171. Combating organized crime requires better international regulatory frameworks and extended efforts in building State capacity in the area of the rule of law. Concerted efforts against human trafficking are also required.

1. Better international regulatory frameworks

172. Several recent international conventions hold the potential to level the playing field by allowing quicker, closer cooperation by States. Such conventions, however, lack universal adherence and suffer from inadequate implementation and observance by participating States. There is a need for mechanisms to monitor Member States' compliance with their commitments and to identify and remedy legislative and institutional deficiencies. The collective response to organized crime depends on the consolidation and strengthening of the international treaty framework. More than half of the Member States of the United Nations have not yet signed or ratified the 2000 United Nations Convention against Transnational Organized Crime and its three Protocols and the 2003 United Nations Convention against Corruption, or adequately resourced the monitoring provisions of these Conventions and Protocols. **Member States that have not signed, ratified or resourced these Conventions and Protocols should do so, and all Member States should support the United Nations Office on Drugs and Crime in its work in this area.**

173. Organized crime groups move freely across borders; legal cooperation is impeded by them. **Member States should establish a central authority to facilitate the exchange of evidence among national judicial authorities, mutual legal assistance among prosecutorial authorities and the implementation of extradition requests.**

174. Unlike terrorists, criminals are motivated by financial gain. The single best strategy for weakening organized crime is to eliminate its ability to launder money. Transnational organized crime generates income of about $500 billion a year, with some sources estimating triple that amount. In 2000, between $500 billion and $1.5 trillion were laundered. Despite the magnitude of these sums and their role in furthering organized crime, many States do not regulate money-laundering. Indiscriminate enforcement of bank secrecy and the rapid development of financial havens remains a serious obstacle to tackling this problem. **A comprehensive international convention on money-laundering that addresses these issues needs to be negotiated, and endorsed by the General Assembly.**

175. The most obscene form taken by organized crime is the traffic in human beings, and all Member States should take decisive action to halt it. **Member States**

should sign and ratify the Protocol to Prevent, Suppress and Punish Trafficking in Persons, Especially Women and Children, and parties to the Protocol should take all necessary steps to effectively implement it.

176. The United Nations should further promote technical cooperation among countries and international law enforcement agencies to secure the protection of and support for victims of trafficking in countries of origin, transit and destination. In particular, the United Nations Office on Drugs and Crime and the International Labour Organization (ILO) should aggressively promote the human rights of women and children, and should integrate specific strategies to assist them into their programmes and help protect them against becoming victims of human trafficking.

2. Better State capacity-building

177. Lagging implementation is also a function, in some cases, of limited State capacity. In order to address this problem international organizations, most prominently the United Nations Office for Drugs and Crime, have set up technical assistance and training programmes aimed at the building of effective national law enforcement and judicial institutions. However, these activities are insufficiently resourced. **The United Nations should establish a robust capacity-building mechanism for rule-of-law assistance.** Regional organizations and multinational financial institutions should actively join these efforts.

VIII. The role of sanctions

178. In dealing preventively with the threats to international peace and security, sanctions are a vital though imperfect tool. They constitute a necessary middle ground between war and words when nations, individuals and rebel groups violate international norms, and where a failure to respond would weaken those norms, embolden other transgressors or be interpreted as consent.

179. Targeted sanctions (financial, travel, aviation or arms embargoes) are useful for putting pressure on leaders and elites with minimal humanitarian consequences, provide a less costly alternative to other options and can be tailored to specific circumstances. By isolating violators of international standards and laws, even modest sanctions measures (including sports embargoes) can serve an important symbolic purpose. The threat of sanctions can be a powerful means of deterrence and prevention.

180. **The Security Council must ensure that sanctions are effectively implemented and enforced:**

(a) When the Security Council imposes a sanctions regime - including arms embargoes - it should routinely establish monitoring mechanisms and provide them with the necessary authority and capacity to carry out high-quality, in-depth investigations. Adequate budgetary provisions must be made to implement those mechanisms;

(b) Security Council sanctions committees should be mandated to develop improved guidelines and reporting procedures to assist States in sanctions implementation, and to improve procedures for maintaining accurate lists of individuals and entities subject to targeted sanctions;

(c) The Secretary-General should appoint a senior official with sufficient supporting resources to enable the Secretary-General to supply the Security Council with analysis of the best way to target sanctions and to assist in coordinating their implementation. This official would also assist compliance efforts; identify technical assistance needs and coordinate such assistance; and make recommendations on any adjustments necessary to enhance the effectiveness of sanctions;

(d) Donors should devote more resources to strengthening the legal, administrative, and policing and border-control capacity of Member States to implement sanctions. These capacity-building measures should include efforts to improve air-traffic interdiction in zones of conflict;

(e) The Security Council should, in instances of verified, chronic violations, impose secondary sanctions against those involved in sanctions-busting;

(f) The Secretary-General, in consultation with the Security Council, should ensure that an appropriate auditing mechanism is in place to oversee sanctions administration.

181. Sanctions committees should improve procedures for providing humanitarian exemptions and routinely conduct assessments of the humanitarian impact of sanctions. The Security Council should continue to strive to mitigate the humanitarian consequences of sanctions.

182. Where sanctions involve lists of individuals or entities, sanctions committees should establish procedures to review the cases of those claiming to have been incorrectly placed or retained on such lists.

Part 3
Collective security and the use of force

Part 3
Collective security and the use of force

Synopsis

What happens if peaceful prevention fails? If none of the preventive measures so far described stop the descent into war and chaos? If distant threats do become imminent? Or if imminent threats become actual? Or if a non-imminent threat nonetheless becomes very real and measures short of the use of military force seem powerless to stop it?

We address here the circumstances in which effective collective security may require the backing of military force, starting with the rules of international law that must govern any decision to go to war, if anarchy is not to prevail. It is necessary to distinguish between situations in which a State claims to act in self-defence; situations in which a State is posing a threat to others outside its borders; and situations in which the threat is primarily internal and the issue is the responsibility to protect a State's own people. In all cases, we believe that the Charter of the United Nations, properly understood and applied, is equal to the task: Article 51 needs neither extension nor restriction of its long-understood scope, and Chapter VII fully empowers the Security Council to deal with every kind of threat that States may confront. The task is not to find alternatives to the Security Council as a source of authority but to make it work better than it has.

That force *can* legally be used, does not always mean that, as a matter of good conscience and good sense, it *should* be used. We identify a set of guidelines - five criteria of legitimacy - which we believe the Security Council (and anyone else involved in these decisions) should always address in considering whether to authorize or apply military force. The adoption of these guidelines (seriousness of threat, proper purpose, last resort, proportional means and balance of consequences) will not produce agreed conclusions with push-button predictability, but should significantly improve the chances of reaching international consensus on what have been in recent years deeply divisive issues.

We also address here the other major issues that arise during and after violent conflict, including the needed capacities for peace enforcement, peacekeeping and peacebuilding, and the protection of civilians. A central recurring theme is the necessity for all members of the international community, developed and developing States alike, to be much more forthcoming in providing and supporting deployable military resources. Empty gestures are all too easy to make: an effective, efficient and equitable collective security system demands real commitment.

IX. Using force: rules and guidelines

183. The framers of the Charter of the United Nations recognized that force may be necessary for the "prevention and removal of threats to the peace, and for the suppression of acts of aggression or other breaches of the peace". Military force, legally and properly applied, is a vital component of any workable system of collective security, whether defined in the traditional narrow sense or more broadly as we would prefer. But few contemporary policy issues cause more difficulty, or involve higher stakes, than the principles concerning its use and application to individual cases.

184. The maintenance of world peace and security depends importantly on there being a common global understanding, and acceptance, of when the application of force is both legal and legitimate. One of these elements being satisfied without the other will always weaken the international legal order - and thereby put both State and human security at greater risk.

A. The question of legality

185. The Charter of the United Nations, in Article 2.4, expressly prohibits Member States from using or threatening force against each other, allowing only two exceptions: self-defence under Article 51, and military measures authorized by the Security Council under Chapter VII (and by extension for regional organizations under Chapter VIII) in response to "any threat to the peace, breach of the peace or act of aggression".

186. For the first 44 years of the United Nations, Member States often violated these rules and used military force literally hundreds of times, with a paralysed Security Council passing very few Chapter VII resolutions and Article 51 only rarely providing credible cover. Since the end of the cold war, however, the yearning for an international system governed by the rule of law has grown. There is little evident international acceptance of the idea of security being best preserved by a balance of power, or by any single - even benignly motivated - superpower.

187. But in seeking to apply the express language of the Charter, three particularly difficult questions arise in practice: first, when a State claims the right to strike preventively, in self-defence, in response to a threat which is not imminent; secondly, when a State appears to be posing an external threat, actual or potential, to other States or people outside its borders, but there is disagreement in the Security Council as to what to do about it; and thirdly, where the threat is primarily internal, to a State's own people.

1. Article 51 of the Charter of the United Nations and self-defence

188.   The language of this article is restrictive: "Nothing in the present Charter shall impair the inherent right of individual or collective self-defense if an armed attack occurs against a member of the United Nations, until the Security Council has taken measures to maintain international peace and security". However, a threatened State, according to long established international law, can take military action as long as the threatened attack is *imminent*, no other means would deflect it and the action is proportionate. The problem arises where the threat in question is not imminent but still claimed to be real: for example the acquisition, with allegedly hostile intent, of nuclear weapons-making capability.

189.   Can a State, without going to the Security Council, claim in these circumstances the right to act, in anticipatory self-defence, not just pre-emptively (against an imminent or proximate threat) but preventively (against a non-imminent or non-proximate one)? Those who say "yes" argue that the potential harm from some threats (e.g., terrorists armed with a nuclear weapon) is so great that one simply cannot risk waiting until they become imminent, and that less harm may be done (e.g., avoiding a nuclear exchange or radioactive fallout from a reactor destruction) by acting earlier.

190.   The short answer is that if there are good arguments for preventive military action, with good evidence to support them, they should be put to the Security Council, which can authorize such action if it chooses to. If it does not so choose, there will be, by definition, time to pursue other strategies, including persuasion, negotiation, deterrence and containment - and to visit again the military option.

191.   For those impatient with such a response, the answer must be that, in a world full of perceived potential threats, the risk to the global order and the norm of non-intervention on which it continues to be based is simply too great for the legality of unilateral preventive action, as distinct from collectively endorsed action, to be accepted. Allowing one to so act is to allow all.

192.   **We do not favour the rewriting or reinterpretation of Article 51.**

2. Chapter VII of the Charter of the United Nations and external threats

193.   In the case of a State posing a threat to other States, people outside its borders or to international order more generally, the language of Chapter VII is inherently broad enough, and has been interpreted broadly enough, to allow the

Security Council to approve any coercive action at all, including military action, against a State when it deems this "necessary to maintain or restore international peace and security". That is the case whether the threat is occurring now, in the imminent future or more distant future; whether it involves the State's own actions or those of non-State actors it harbours or supports; or whether it takes the form of an act or omission, an actual or potential act of violence or simply a challenge to the Council's authority.

194. We emphasize that the concerns we expressed about the legality of the preventive use of military force in the case of self-defence under Article 51 are not applicable in the case of collective action authorized under Chapter VII. In the world of the twenty-first century, the international community does have to be concerned about nightmare scenarios combining terrorists, weapons of mass destruction and irresponsible States, and much more besides, which may conceivably justify the use of force, not just reactively but preventively and before a latent threat becomes imminent. The question is not whether such action can be taken: it can, by the Security Council as the international community's collective security voice, at any time it deems that there is a threat to international peace and security. The Council may well need to be prepared to be much more proactive on these issues, taking more decisive action earlier, than it has been in the past.

195. Questions of legality apart, there will be issues of prudence, or legitimacy, about whether such preventive action *should* be taken: crucial among them is whether there is credible evidence of the reality of the threat in question (taking into account both capability and specific intent) and whether the military response is the only reasonable one in the circumstances. We address these issues further below.

196. It may be that some States will always feel that they have the obligation to their own citizens, and the capacity, to do whatever they feel they need to do, unburdened by the constraints of collective Security Council process. But however understandable that approach may have been in the cold war years, when the United Nations was manifestly not operating as an effective collective security system, the world has now changed and expectations about legal compliance are very much higher.

197. One of the reasons why States may want to bypass the Security Council is a lack of confidence in the quality and objectivity of its decision-making. The Council's decisions have often been less than consistent, less than persuasive and less than fully responsive to very real State and human security needs. But the solution is not to reduce the Council to impotence and irrelevance: it is to work from within to reform it, including in the ways we propose in the present report.

198. The Security Council is fully empowered under Chapter VII of the Charter of the United Nations to address the full range of security threats with which States are concerned. The task is not to find alternatives to the Security Council as a source of authority but to make the Council work better than it has.

3. Chapter VII of the Charter of the United Nations, internal threats and the responsibility to protect

199. The Charter of the United Nations is not as clear as it could be when it comes to saving lives within countries in situations of mass atrocity. It "reaffirm(s) faith in fundamental human rights" but does not do much to protect them, and Article 2.7 prohibits intervention "in matters which are essentially within the jurisdiction of any State". There has been, as a result, a long-standing argument in the international community between those who insist on a "right to intervene" in man-made catastrophes and those who argue that the Security Council, for all its powers under Chapter VII to "maintain or restore international security", is prohibited from authorizing any coercive action against sovereign States for whatever happens within their borders.

> *The principle of non-intervention in internal affairs cannot be used to protect genocidal acts or large-scale violations of international humanitarian law or large-scale ethnic cleansing*

200. Under the Convention on the Prevention and Punishment of the Crime of Genocide (Genocide Convention), States have agreed that genocide, whether committed in time of peace or in time of war, is a crime under international law which they undertake to prevent and punish. Since then it has been understood that genocide anywhere is a threat to the security of all and should never be tolerated. The principle of non-intervention in internal affairs cannot be used to protect genocidal acts or other atrocities, such as large-scale violations of international humanitarian law or large-scale ethnic cleansing, which can properly be considered a threat to international security and as such provoke action by the Security Council.

201. The successive humanitarian disasters in Somalia, Bosnia and Herzegovina, Rwanda, Kosovo and now Darfur, Sudan, have concentrated attention not on the immunities of sovereign Governments but their responsibilities, both to their own people and to the wider international community. There is a growing recognition that the issue is not the "right to intervene" of any State, but the "responsibility to protect" of *every* State when it comes to people suffering from avoidable catastrophe - mass murder and rape, ethnic cleansing by forcible expulsion and terror, and deliberate starvation and exposure to disease. And there is a growing acceptance

that while sovereign Governments have the primary responsibility to protect their own citizens from such catastrophes, when they are unable or unwilling to do so that responsibility should be taken up by the wider international community - with it spanning a continuum involving prevention, response to violence, if necessary, and rebuilding shattered societies. The primary focus should be on assisting the cessation of violence through mediation and other tools and the protection of people through such measures as the dispatch of humanitarian, human rights and police missions. Force, if it needs to be used, should be deployed as a last resort.

202. The Security Council so far has been neither very consistent nor very effective in dealing with these cases, very often acting too late, too hesitantly or not at all. But step by step, the Council and the wider international community have come to accept that, under Chapter VII and in pursuit of the emerging norm of a collective international responsibility to protect, it can always authorize military action to redress catastrophic internal wrongs if it is prepared to declare that the situation is a "threat to international peace and security", not especially difficult when breaches of international law are involved.

203. **We endorse the emerging norm that there is a collective international responsibility to protect, exercisable by the Security Council authorizing military intervention as a last resort, in the event of genocide and other large-scale killing, ethnic cleansing or serious violations of international humanitarian law which sovereign Governments have proved powerless or unwilling to prevent.**

B. The question of legitimacy

204. The effectiveness of the global collective security system, as with any other legal order, depends ultimately not only on the legality of decisions but also on the common perception of their legitimacy - their being made on solid evidentiary grounds, and for the right reasons, morally as well as legally.

205. If the Security Council is to win the respect it must have as the primary body in the collective security system, it is critical that its most important and influential decisions, those with large-scale life-and-death impact, be better made, better substantiated and better communicated. In particular, in deciding whether or not to authorize the use of force, the Council should adopt and systematically address a set of agreed guidelines, going directly not to whether force *can* legally be used but whether, as a matter of good conscience and good sense, it *should* be.

206. The guidelines we propose will not produce agreed conclusions with push-button predictability. The point of adopting them is not to guarantee that the

objectively best outcome will always prevail. It is rather to maximize the possibility of achieving Security Council consensus around when it is appropriate or not to use coercive action, including armed force; to maximize international support for whatever the Security Council decides; and to minimize the possibility of individual Member States bypassing the Security Council.

207. In considering whether to authorize or endorse the use of military force, the Security Council should always address - whatever other considerations it may take into account - at least the following five basic criteria of legitimacy:

(a) *Seriousness of threat.* Is the threatened harm to State or human security of a kind, and sufficiently clear and serious, to justify *prima facie* the use of military force? In the case of internal threats, does it involve genocide and other large-scale killing, ethnic cleansing or serious violations of international humanitarian law, actual or imminently apprehended?

(b) *Proper purpose.* Is it clear that the primary purpose of the proposed military action is to halt or avert the threat in question, whatever other purposes or motives may be involved?

(c) *Last resort.* Has every non-military option for meeting the threat in question been explored, with reasonable grounds for believing that other measures will not succeed?

(d) *Proportional means.* Are the scale, duration and intensity of the proposed military action the minimum necessary to meet the threat in question?

(e) *Balance of consequences.* Is there a reasonable chance of the military action being successful in meeting the threat in question, with the consequences of action not likely to be worse than the consequences of inaction?

208. The above guidelines for authorizing the use of force should be embodied in declaratory resolutions of the Security Council and General Assembly.

209. We also believe it would be valuable if individual Member States, whether or not they are members of the Security Council, subscribed to them.

X. Peace enforcement and peacekeeping capability

210. When the Security Council makes a determination that force must be authorized, questions remain about the capacities at its disposal to implement that decision. In recent years, decisions to authorize military force for the purpose of enforcing the peace have primarily fallen to multinational forces. Blue helmet

peacekeepers - in United Nations uniform and under direct United Nations command - have more frequently been deployed when forces are authorized with the consent of the parties to conflict, to help implement a peace agreement or monitor ceasefire lines after combat.

211. Discussion of the necessary capacities has been confused by the tendency to refer to peacekeeping missions as "Chapter VI operations" and peace enforcement missions as "Chapter VII operations" - meaning consent-based or coercion-based, respectively. This shorthand is also often used to distinguish missions that do not involve the use of deadly force for purposes other than self-defence, and those that do.

212. Both characterizations are to some extent misleading. There *is* a distinction between operations in which the robust use of force is integral to the mission from the outset (e.g., responses to cross-border invasions or an explosion of violence, in which the recent practice has been to mandate multinational forces) and operations in which there is a reasonable expectation that force may not be needed at all (e.g., traditional peacekeeping missions monitoring and verifying a ceasefire or those assisting in implementing peace agreements, where blue helmets are still the norm).

213. But both kinds of operation need the authorization of the Security Council (Article 51 self-defence cases apart), and in peacekeeping cases as much as in peace-enforcement cases it is now the usual practice for a Chapter VII mandate to be given (even if that is not always welcomed by troop contributors). This is on the basis that even the most benign environment can turn sour - when spoilers emerge to undermine a peace agreement and put civilians at risk - and that it is desirable for there to be complete certainty about the mission's capacity to respond with force, if necessary. On the other hand, the difference between Chapter VI and VII mandates can be exaggerated: there is little doubt that peacekeeping missions operating under Chapter VI (and thus operating without enforcement powers) have the right to use force in self-defence - and this right is widely understood to extend to "defence of the mission".

214. The real challenge, in any deployment of forces of any configuration with any role, is to ensure that they have (a) an appropriate, clear and well understood mandate, applicable to all the changing circumstances that might reasonably be envisaged, and (b) all the necessary resources to implement that mandate fully.

215. The demand for personnel for both full-scale peace-enforcement missions and peacekeeping missions remains higher than the ready supply. At the end of 2004, there are more than 60,000 peacekeepers deployed in 16 missions around the world. If international efforts stay on track to end several long-standing wars in Africa, the numbers of peacekeepers needed will soon substantially increase. In the

absence of a commensurate increase in available personnel, United Nations peace-keeping risks repeating some of its worst failures of the 1990s.

216. At present, the total global supply of personnel is constrained both by the fact that the armed forces of many countries remain configured for cold war duties, with less than 10 per cent of those in uniform available for active deployment at any given time, and by the fact that few nations have sufficient transport and logistic capabilities to move and supply those who are available. For peace-keeping, and in extreme cases peace enforcement, to continue to be an effective and accepted instrument of collective security, the availability of peacekeepers must grow. **The developed States have particular responsibilities here, and should do more to transform their existing force capacities into suitable contingents for peace operations.**

217. Prompt and effective response to today's challenges requires a dependable capacity for the rapid deployment of personnel and equipment for peacekeeping and law enforcement. States that have either global or regional air- or sea-lift capacities should make these available to the United Nations, either free of charge or on the basis of a negotiated fee-based structure for the reimbursement of the additional costs associated with United Nations use of these capacities.

218. **Member States should strongly support the efforts of the Department of Peacekeeping Operations of the United Nations Secretariat, building on the important work of the Panel on United Nations Peace Operations (see A/55/305-S/2000/809), to improve its use of strategic deployment stockpiles, standby arrangements, trust funds and other mechanisms to meet the tighter deadlines necessary for effective deployment.**

219. However, it is unlikely that the demand for rapid action will be met through United Nations mechanisms alone. We welcome the European Union decision to establish standby high readiness, self-sufficient battalions that can reinforce United Nations missions. **Others with advanced military capacities should be encouraged to develop similar capacities at up to brigade level and to place them at the disposal of the United Nations.**

Regional cooperation

220. Since the mid-1990s, there has been a trend towards a variety of regional- and subregional-based peacekeeping missions. This trend holds the promise of developing regional capacity to address shortfalls in the numbers of peacekeepers, and it should augment and not detract from the ability of the United Nations to respond when blue helmets are requested. This poses a challenge for the Security Council and regional organizations to work closely with each other

and mutually support each other's efforts to keep the peace and ensure that regional operations are accountable to universally accepted human rights standards. We address this question in part four below.

XI. Post-conflict peacebuilding

A. The role of peacekeepers

221. It is often necessary to build confidence among former adversaries and provide security to ordinary people trying to rebuild their lives and communities after conflict. The mediation and successful implementation of a peace agreement offers hope for breaking long-standing cycles of violence that haunt many war-inflicted countries. Resources spent on implementation of peace agreements and peacebuilding are one of the best investments that can be made for conflict prevention - States that have experienced civil war face a high risk of recurrence.

> *Resources spent on implementation of peace agreements and peacebuilding are one of the best investments that can be made for conflict prevention*

222. Implementing peace agreements to end civil wars poses unique challenges for peacekeepers. Unlike inter-State wars, making peace in civil war requires overcoming daunting security dilemmas. Spoilers, factions who see a peace agreement as inimical to their interest, power or ideology, use violence to undermine or overthrow settlements. Peacekeeping fails when resources and strategies are not commensurate to meeting the challenge they pose - as occurred repeatedly in the 1990s, for example in Rwanda and Sierra Leone. When peacekeeping operations are deployed to implement peace agreements, they must be equipped to repel attacks from spoilers. Contingency plans for responding to hostile opposition should be an integral part of the mission design; missions that do not have the troop strength to resist aggression will invite it. In some contexts, opposition to a peace agreement is not tactical but fundamental. We must learn the lesson: peace agreements by Governments or rebels that engage in or encourage mass human rights abuses have no value and cannot be implemented. These contexts are not appropriate for consent-based peacekeeping; rather, they must be met with concerted action. **The Secretary-General should recommend and the Security Council should authorize troop strengths sufficient to deter and repel hostile factions.**

223. Most peacekeeping situations also require policing and other law and order functions, and the slow deployment of police contingents has marred successive operations. **The United Nations should have a small corps of senior police officers and managers (50-100 personnel) who could undertake mission**

assessments and organize the start-up of police components of peace operations, and the General Assembly should authorize this capacity.

B. The larger peacebuilding task

224. Deploying peace enforcement and peacekeeping forces may be essential in terminating conflicts but are not sufficient for long-term recovery. Serious attention to the longer-term process of peacebuilding in all its multiple dimensions is critical; failure to invest adequately in peacebuilding increases the odds that a country will relapse into conflict.

225. In both the period before the outbreak of civil war and in the transition out of war, neither the United Nations nor the broader international community, including the international financial institutions, are well organized to assist countries attempting to build peace. When peacekeepers leave a country, it falls off the radar screen of the Security Council. While the Economic and Social Council has created

> *When peacekeepers leave a country, it falls off the radar screen of the Security Council.*

several ad hoc committees to address specific cases, results have proven mixed and even the proponents of these committees acknowledge that they have not succeeded in generating crucial resources to assist fragile transitions. What is needed is a single intergovernmental organ dedicated to peacebuilding, empowered to monitor and pay close attention to countries at risk, ensure concerted action by donors, agencies, programmes and financial institutions, and mobilize financial resources for sustainable peace. We address this need in part four below.

226. Similarly, at the field level, many different elements of the United Nations system and the broader international community engage in some form of peacebuilding, but they work too slowly and without adequate coordination. Effective coordination is critical. National authorities should be at the heart of this coordination effort, and should be supported by coherent United Nations and international presences. Robust donor coordination mechanisms at the field level, involving Governments, bilateral donors, the international financial institutions and the United Nations coordinator (special representative of the Secretary-General or resident coordinator) representing the United Nations funds, programmes and agencies, have proved their value for ensuring effective peacebuilding. **Special representatives should have the authority and guidance to work with relevant parties to establish such mechanisms, as well as the resources to perform coordination functions effectively, including ensuring that the sequencing of United Nations assessments and activities is consistent with Government priorities.**

227. Given that many peace operations can expect resource shortfalls, the efficient use of resources is all the more important. Demobilizing combatants is the single most important factor determining the success of peace operations. Without demobilization, civil wars cannot be brought to an end and other critical goals - such as democratization, justice and development - have little chance for success. In case after case, however, demobilization is not accorded priority by funders. When peace operations are deployed, they must be resourced to undertake the demobilization and disarmament of combatants; this is a priority for successful peace implementation. These tasks should be integrated into the assessed budget of peacekeeping operations, under the authority of the head of mission. **The Security Council should mandate and the General Assembly should authorize funding for disarmament and demobilization programmes from assessed budgets.**

228. But these programmes will be ineffective without the provision of resources for reintegration and rehabilitation. Failure to successfully implement such programmes will result in youth unemployment and fuel the development of criminal gangs and violence and ultimately a relapse into conflict. **A standing fund for peacebuilding should be established at the level of at least $250 million that can be used to finance the recurrent expenditures of a nascent Government, as well as critical agency programmes in the areas of rehabilitation and reintegration.**

229. Along with establishing security, the core task of peacebuilding is to build effective public institutions that, through negotiations with civil society, can establish a consensual framework for governing within the rule of law. Relatively cheap investments in civilian security through police, judicial and rule-of-law reform, local capacity-building for human rights and reconciliation, and local capacity-building for public sector service delivery can greatly benefit long-term peacebuilding. This should be reflected in the policies of the United Nations, international financial institutions and donors, and should be given priority in long-term policy and funding.

230. To address this task, United Nations field representatives (including heads of peacekeeping operations) require dedicated support on the broader aspects of peacebuilding strategy, especially in the area of rule of law. The creation of a Peacebuilding Support Office (see part four below) would address this need.

XII. Protecting civilians

231. In many civil wars, combatants target civilians and relief workers with impunity. Beyond direct violence, deaths from starvation, disease and the collapse of public health dwarf the numbers killed by bullets and bombs. Millions

more are displaced internally or across borders. Human rights abuses and gender violence are rampant.

232. Under international law, the primary responsibility to protect civilians from suffering in war lies with belligerents - State or non-State. International humanitarian law provides minimum protection and standards applicable to the most vulnerable in situations of armed conflict, including women, children and refugees, and must be respected.

233. **All combatants must abide by the provisions of the Geneva Conventions. All Member States should sign, ratify and act on all treaties relating to the protection of civilians, such as the Genocide Convention, the Geneva Conventions, the Rome Statute of the International Criminal Court and all refugee conventions.**

Particularly egregious violations, such as occur when armed groups militarize refugee camps, require emphatic responses from the international community, including from the Security Council

234. Humanitarian aid is a vital tool for helping Governments to fulfil this responsibility. Its core purpose is to protect civilian victims, minimize their suffering and keep them alive during the conflict so that when war ends they have the opportunity to rebuild shattered lives. The provision of assistance is a necessary part of this effort. Donors must fully and equitably fund humanitarian protection and assistance operations.

235. The Secretary-General, based in part on work undertaken by the United Nations High Commissioner for Refugees and strong advocacy efforts by non-governmental organizations, has prepared a 10-point platform for action for the protection of civilians in armed conflict. The Secretary-General's 10-point platform for action should be considered by all actors - States, NGOs and international organizations - in their efforts to protect civilians in armed conflict.

236. From this platform, particular attention should be placed on the question of access to civilians, which is routinely and often flagrantly denied. United Nations humanitarian field staff, as well as United Nations political and peace-keeping representatives, should be well trained and well supported to negotiate access. Such efforts also require better coordination of bilateral initiatives. The Security Council can use field missions and other diplomatic measures to enhance access to and protection of civilians.

237. Particularly egregious violations, such as occur when armed groups militarize refugee camps, require emphatic responses from the international community, including from the Security Council acting under Chapter VII of the Charter of the United Nations. Although the Security Council has acknowledged that such militarization is a threat to peace and security, it has not developed the

capacity or shown the will to confront the problem. **The Security Council should fully implement resolution 1265 (1999) on the protection of civilians in armed conflict.**

238. Of special concern is the use of sexual violence as a weapon of conflict. The human rights components of peacekeeping operations should be given explicit mandates and sufficient resources to investigate and report on human rights violations against women. Security Council resolution 1325 (2000) on women, peace and security and the associated Independent Experts' Assessment provide important additional recommendations for the protection of women. **The Security Council, United Nations agencies and Member States should fully implement its recommendations.**

United Nations staff security

239. The ability of the United Nations to protect civilians and help end conflict is directly related to United Nations staff security, which has been eroding since the mid-1990s. To be able to maintain presence, and operate securely and effectively, the United Nations needs four things: the capacity to perform its mandated tasks fully; freedom from unwarranted intrusion by Member States into operations; full respect by staff of United Nations codes of impartiality; and a professional security service, with access to Member States' intelligence and threat assessments. The Secretary-General has recommended the creation of such a service, headed by a Director who will report directly to him. **Member States should support and fully fund the proposed Directorate of Security and accord high priority to assisting the Secretary-General in implementing a new staff security system in 2005.**

Part 4
A more effective United Nations for the twenty-first century

Part 4
A more effective United Nations for the twenty-first century

Synopsis

The United Nations was never intended to be a utopian exercise. It was meant to be a collective security system that worked. The Charter of the United Nations provided the most powerful States with permanent membership on the Security Council and the veto. In exchange, they were expected to use their power for the common good and promote and obey international law. As Harry Truman, then President of the United States, noted in his speech to the final plenary session of the founding conference of the United Nations Organization, "we all have to recognize - no matter how great our strength - that we must deny ourselves the license to do always as we please".

In approaching the issue of United Nations reform, it is as important today as it was in 1945 to combine power with principle. Recommendations that ignore underlying power realities will be doomed to failure or irrelevance, but recommendations that simply reflect raw distributions of power and make no effort to bolster international principles are unlikely to gain the widespread adherence required to shift international behaviour.

Proposed changes should be driven by real-world need. Change for its own sake is likely to run the well-worn course of the endless reform debates of the past decade. The litmus test is this: does a proposed change help meet the challenge posed by a virulent threat?

Throughout the Panel's work, we have looked for institutional weaknesses in current responses to threats. The following stand as the most urgently in need of remedy:

- The General Assembly has lost vitality and often fails to focus effectively on the most compelling issues of the day.
- The Security Council will need to be more proactive in the future. For this to happen, those who contribute most to the Organization financially, militarily and diplomatically should participate more in Council decision-making, and those who participate in Council decision-making should contribute more to the Organization. The Security Council needs greater credibility, legitimacy and representation to do all that we demand of it.
- There is a major institutional gap in addressing countries under stress and countries emerging from conflict. Such countries often suffer from attention, policy guidance and resource deficits.

- The Security Council has not made the most of the potential advantages of working with regional and subregional organizations.
- There must be new institutional arrangements to address the economic and social threats to international security.
- The Commission on Human Rights suffers from a legitimacy deficit that casts doubts on the overall reputation of the United Nations.
- There is a need for a more professional and better organized Secretariat that is much more capable of concerted action.

The reforms we propose will not by themselves make the United Nations more effective. In the absence of Member States reaching agreement on the security consensus contained in the present report, the United Nations will underachieve. Its institutions will still only be as strong as the energy, resources and attention devoted to them by Member States and their leaders.

XIII. The General Assembly

240. The General Assembly is, first and foremost, a universal body, representing almost every State in the world. Its unique legitimacy must be used to move us towards global consensus on the policy issues of greatest contemporary importance. We cannot overestimate the importance of holding a general debate every year in which the view of every Government is presented, providing a crucial opportunity to gauge the pulse of the international community. The General Assembly provides a unique forum in which to forge consensus. **Members should use the opportunity provided by the Millennium Review Summit in 2005 to forge a new consensus on broader, more effective collective security.**

241. The keys to strengthening the General Assembly's role are focus and structure. Its norm-making capacity is often squandered on debates about minutiae or thematic topics outpaced by real-world events. Its inability to reach closure on issues undermines its relevance. An unwieldy and static agenda leads to repetitive debates. Although some resolutions, such as the 1948 Universal Declaration of Human Rights and the 2000 United Nations Millennium Declaration, are highly significant, many others are repetitive, obscure or inapplicable, thus diminishing the credibility of the body. But detailed procedural fixes are not going to make the General Assembly a more effective instrument than it is now. That can only be achieved if its members show a sustained determination to put behind them the approach which they have applied hitherto.

242. **Member States should renew efforts to enable the General Assembly to perform its function as the main deliberative organ of the United Nations. This requires a better conceptualization and shortening of the agenda, which should reflect the contemporary challenges facing the international**

community. Smaller, more tightly focused committees could help sharpen and improve resolutions that are brought to the whole Assembly.

243. We believe that civil society and non-governmental organizations can provide valuable knowledge and perspectives on global issues. **We endorse the recommendation of the recently released report of the Panel of Eminent Persons on United Nations-Civil Society Relations (see A/58/817) that the General Assembly should establish a better mechanism to enable systematic engagement with civil society organizations.**

XIV. The Security Council

244. The founders of the United Nations conferred primary responsibility on the Security Council for the maintenance of international peace and security. The Security Council was designed to enable the world body to act decisively to prevent and remove threats. It was created to be not just a representative but a responsible body, one that had the capacity for decisive action. The five permanent members were given veto rights but were also expected to shoulder an extra burden in promoting global security. Article 23 of the Charter of the United Nations established that membership in the Council as a whole was explicitly linked not just to geographical balance but also to contributions to maintaining peace and security.

245. Since the Council was formed the threats and challenges to international peace and security have changed, as has the distribution of power among members. But the Security Council has been slow to change. Decisions cannot be implemented just by members of the Security Council but require extensive military, financial and political involvement by other States. Decisions taken and mandates given have often lacked the essential components of realism, adequate resources and the political determination to see them through. The Secretary-General is frequently holding out a begging bowl to implement Security Council decisions. Moreover, the paucity of representation from the broad membership diminishes support for Security Council decisions.

246. Since the end of the cold war, the effectiveness of the Council has improved, as has its willingness to act; but it has not always been equitable in its actions, nor has it acted consistently or effectively in the face of genocide or other atrocities. This has gravely damaged its credibility. The financial and military contributions to the United Nations of some of the five permanent members are modest compared to their special status, and often the Council's non-permanent members have been unable to make the necessary contribution to the work of the Organization envisaged by the Charter. Even outside the use of a formal veto, the ability of the five permanent members to keep critical issues of peace and security off the Security Council's agenda has further undermined confidence in the body's work.

247. Yet recent experience has also shown that the Security Council is the body in the United Nations most capable of organizing action and responding rapidly to new threats.

248. Thus, the challenge for any reform is to increase both the effectiveness and the credibility of the Security Council and, most importantly, to enhance its capacity and willingness to act in the face of threats. This requires greater involvement in Security Council decision-making by those who contribute most; greater contributions from those with special decision-making authority; and greater consultation with those who must implement its decisions. It also requires a firm consensus on the nature of today's threats, on the obligations of broadened collective security, on the necessity of prevention, and on when and why the Council should authorize the use of force.

> *... the challenge for any reform is to increase both the effectiveness and the credibility of the Security Council and, most importantly, to enhance its capacity and willingness to act in the face of threats*

249. We believe that reforms of the Security Council should meet the following principles:

    (a) They should, in honouring Article 23 of the Charter of the United Nations, increase the involvement in decision-making of those who contribute most to the United Nations financially, militarily and diplomatically - specifically in terms of contributions to United Nations assessed budgets, participation in mandated peace operations, contributions to voluntary activities of the United Nations in the areas of security and development, and diplomatic activities in support of United Nations objectives and mandates. Among developed countries, achieving or making substantial progress towards the internationally agreed level of 0.7 per cent of GNP for ODA should be considered an important criterion of contribution;

    (b) They should bring into the decision-making process countries more representative of the broader membership, especially of the developing world;

    (c) They should not impair the effectiveness of the Security Council;

    (d) They should increase the democratic and accountable nature of the body.

250. The Panel believes that a decision on the enlargement of the Council, satisfying these criteria, is now a necessity. The presentation of two clearly defined alternatives, of the kind described below as models A and B, should help to clarify - and perhaps bring to resolution - a debate which has made little progress in the last 12 years.

251. Models A and B both involve a distribution of seats as between four major regional areas, which we identify respectively as "Africa", "Asia and Pacific", "Europe" and "Americas". We see these descriptions as helpful in making and implementing judgements about the composition of the Security Council, but make no recommendation about changing the composition of the current regional groups for general electoral and other United Nations purposes. Some members of the Panel, in particular our Latin American colleagues, expressed a preference for basing any distribution of seats on the current regional groups.

252. Model A provides for six new permanent seats, with no veto being created, and three new two-year term non-permanent seats, divided among the major regional areas as follows:

Regional area	Number of States	Permanent seats (continuing)	Proposed new permanent seats	Proposed two-year seats (non-renewable)	Total
Africa	53	0	2	4	6
Asia and Pacific	56	1	2	3	6
Europe	47	3	1	2	6
Americas	35	1	1	4	6
Totals model A	191	5	6	13	24

253. Model B provides for no new permanent seats but creates a new category of eight four-year renewable-term seats and one new two-year non-permanent (and non-renewable) seat, divided among the major regional areas as follows:

Regional area	Number of States	Permanent seats (continuing)	Proposed four-year renewable seats	Proposed two-year seats (non-renewable)	Total
Africa	53	0	2	4	6
Asia and Pacific	56	1	2	3	6
Europe	47	3	2	1	6
Americas	35	1	2	3	6
Totals model B	191	5	8	11	24

254. In both models, having regard to Article 23 of the Charter of the United Nations, a method of encouraging Member States to contribute more to international peace and security would be for the General Assembly, taking into account established practices of regional consultation, to elect Security Council members by giving preference for permanent or longer-term seats to those States that are among the top three financial contributors in their relevant regional area to the regular budget, or the top three voluntary contributors from their regional area, or the top three troop contributors from their regional area to United Nations peacekeeping missions.

255. The Panel was strongly of the view that no change to the composition of the Security Council should itself be regarded as permanent or unchallengeable in the future. Therefore, there should be a review of the composition of the Security Council in 2020, including, in this context, a review of the contribution (as defined in para. 249 above) of permanent and non-permanent members from the point of view of the Council's effectiveness in taking collective action to prevent and remove new and old threats to international peace and security.

256. Neither model involves any expansion of the veto or any Charter modification of the Security Council's existing powers. We recognize that the veto had an important function in reassuring the United Nations most powerful members that their interests would be safeguarded. We see no practical way of changing the existing members' veto powers. Yet, as a whole the institution of the veto has an anachronistic character that is unsuitable for the institution in an increasingly democratic age and we would urge that its use be limited to matters where vital interests are genuinely at stake. We also ask the permanent members, in their individual capacities, to pledge themselves to refrain from the use of the veto in cases of genocide and large-scale human rights abuses. We recommend that under any reform proposal, there should be no expansion of the veto.

257. We propose the introduction of a system of "indicative voting", whereby members of the Security Council could call for a public indication of positions on a proposed action. Under this indicative vote, "no" votes would not have a veto effect, nor would the final tally of the vote have any legal force. The second formal vote on any resolution would take place under the current procedures of the Council. This would, we believe, increase the accountability of the veto function.

258. In recent years, many informal improvements have been made to the transparency and accountability of the Security Council's deliberative and decision-making procedures. We also remind the Security Council that troop contribu-

tors have rights under Article 44 of the Charter to be fully consulted concerning the deployment of troops to Council-mandated operations. **We recommend that processes to improve transparency and accountability be incorporated and formalized in the Council's rules of procedure.**

259. Many delegations on the Security Council lack access to professional military advice. Yet they are frequently called upon to take decisions with far-ranging military implications. We recommend therefore that the Secretary General's Military Adviser and the members of his staff be available on demand by the Security Council to offer technical and professional advice on military options.

260. We welcome greater civil society engagement in the work of the Security Council.

XV. A Peacebuilding Commission

261. Our analysis has identified a key institutional gap: there is no place in the United Nations system explicitly designed to avoid State collapse and the slide to war or to assist countries in their transition from war to peace. That this was not included in the Charter of the United Nations is no surprise since the work of the United Nations in largely internal conflicts is fairly recent. But today, in an era when dozens of States are under stress or recovering from conflict, there is a clear international obligation to assist States in developing their capacity to perform their sovereign functions effectively and responsibly.

262. The United Nations unique role in this area arises from its international legitimacy; the impartiality of its personnel; its ability to draw on personnel with broad cultural understanding and experience of a wide range of administrative systems, including in the developing world; and its recent experience in organizing transitional administration and transitional authority operations.

263. Strengthening the United Nations capacity for peacebuilding in the widest sense must be a priority for the organization. The United Nations needs to be able to act in a coherent and effective way throughout a whole continuum that runs from early warning through preventive action to post-conflict peacebuilding. **We recommend that the Security Council, acting under Article 29 of the Charter of the United Nations and after consultation with the Economic and Social Council, establish a Peacebuilding Commission.**

264. **The core functions of the Peacebuilding Commission should be to identify countries which are under stress and risk sliding towards State collapse; to organize, in partnership with the national Government, proactive assistance in preventing that process from developing further; to assist in the planning for transitions between conflict and post-conflict**

peacebuilding; and in particular to marshal and sustain the efforts of the international community in post-conflict peacebuilding over whatever period may be necessary.

265. While the precise composition, procedures, and reporting lines of the Peacebuilding Commission will need to be established, they should take account of the following guidelines:

(a) The Peacebuilding Commission should be reasonably small;

(b) It should meet in different configurations, to consider both general policy issues and country-by-country strategies;

(c) It should be chaired for at least one year and perhaps longer by a member approved by the Security Council;

(d) In addition to representation from the Security Council, it should include representation from the Economic and Social Council;

(e) National representatives of the country under consideration should be invited to attend;

(f) The Managing Director of the International Monetary Fund, the President of the World Bank and, when appropriate, heads of regional development banks should be represented at its meetings by appropriate senior officials;

(g) Representatives of the principal donor countries and, when appropriate, the principal troop contributors should be invited to participate in its deliberations;

(h) Representatives of regional and subregional organizations should be invited to participate in its deliberations when such organizations are actively involved in the country in question.

Peacebuilding Support Office

266. A Peacebuilding Support Office should be established in the Secretariat to give the Peacebuilding Commission appropriate Secretariat support and to ensure that the Secretary-General is able to integrate system-wide peacebuilding policies and strategies, develop best practices and provide cohesive support for field operations.

267. The Office should comprise about 20 or more staff of different backgrounds in the United Nations system and with significant experience in peacebuilding strategy and operations. In addition to supporting the Secretary-General and the Peacebuilding Commission, the Office could also, on request, provide assistance and advice to the heads of peace operations, United Nations resident coordinators or national Governments - for example in developing strategies for

transitional political arrangements or building new State institutions. It should submit twice-yearly early warning analyses to the Peacebuilding Commission to help it in organizing its work.

268. The Peacebuilding Support Office should also maintain rosters of national and international experts, particularly those with experience in post-conflict cases.

269. The Office should have an inter-agency advisory board, headed by the Chair of the United Nations Development Group, that would ensure that the Office worked in effective cooperation with other elements of the system that provide related support.

XVI. Regional organizations

270. The ability of the Security Council to become more proactive in preventing and responding to threats will be strengthened by making fuller and more productive use of the Chapter VIII provisions of the Charter of the United Nations than has hitherto been the case.

271. Since the establishment of the United Nations, a considerable number of regional and subregional groupings have been established. Some of these groupings have made important contributions to the stability and prosperity of their members, and some of them have begun to address directly threats to peace and security. We believe the United Nations should encourage the establishment of such groupings, particularly in highly vulnerable parts of the world where no effective security organizations currently exist.

272. Recent experience has demonstrated that regional organizations can be a vital part of the multilateral system. Their efforts need not contradict United Nations efforts, nor do they absolve the United Nations of its primary responsibilities for peace and security. The key is to organize regional action within the framework of the Charter and the purposes of the United Nations, and to ensure that the United Nations and any regional organization with which it works do so in a more integrated fashion than has up to now occurred. This will require that:

   (a) **Authorization from the Security Council should in all cases be sought for regional peace operations**, recognizing that in some urgent situations that authorization may be sought after such operations have commenced;

   (b) **Consultation and cooperation between the United Nations and regional organizations should be expanded and could be formalized in an agreement, covering such issues as meetings of the heads of the organizations, more frequent exchange of information and early warning, co-training of civilian and military personnel, and exchange of personnel within peace** operations;

(c) In the case of African regional and subregional capacities, donor countries should commit to a 10-year process of sustained capacity-building support, within the African Union strategic framework;

(d) Regional organizations that have a capacity for conflict prevention or peacekeeping should place such capacities in the framework of the United Nations Standby Arrangements System;

(e) Member States should agree to allow the United Nations to provide equipment support from United Nations-owned sources to regional operations, as needed;

(f) The rules for the United Nations peacekeeping budget should be amended to give the United Nations the option on a case-by-case basis to finance regional operations authorized by the Security Council with assessed contributions.

273. In recent years, such alliance organizations as NATO (which have not usually been considered regional organizations within the meaning of Chapter VIII of the Charter but have some similar characteristics) have undertaken peacekeeping operations beyond their mandated areas. We welcome this so long as these operations are authorized by and accountable to the Security Council. In the case of NATO, there may also be a constructive role for it to play in assisting in the training and equipping of less well resourced regional organizations and States.

XVII. The Economic and Social Council

274. The framers of the Charter of the United Nations understood that peace and security were inseparable from economic development. The institutional problem we face is twofold: first, decision-making on international economic matters, particularly in the areas of finance and trade, has long left the United Nations and no amount of institutional reform will bring it back; and second, the Charter allowed for the creation of specialized agencies independent of the principal United Nations organs, reducing the role of the Economic and Social Council to one of coordination. The fragmentation of the United Nations funds, programmes and agencies makes this a difficult proposition in the best of times. It would not, however, be realistic to aim for the Economic and Social Council to become the centre of the world's decision-making on matters of trade and finance, or to direct the programmes of the specialized agencies or the international financial institutions.

275. And yet the United Nations does have potential assets in the areas of economic and social development. First, the United Nations is the only place where the issues of peace, security and development can be addressed together at the global

level. Second, the United Nations has an unrivalled convening power, on the basis of which the General Assembly and the major conferences and summits it has convened in the last three decades have generated consensus around internationally accepted goals, especially in the social field. Third, the United Nations shows that it has strong grass-roots support for its goals and can thus mobilize public opinion in their favour. **Three strategies can help the Economic and Social Council enhance its relevance and contribution to collective security, building on United Nations comparative advantages, as described below.**

276. **First, the Economic and Social Council can provide normative and analytical leadership** in a time of much debate about the causes of, and interconnections between, the many threats we face. To that end:

    (a) **We recommend that the Economic and Social Council establish a Committee on the Social and Economic Aspects of Security Threats,** and that it use its powers to commission research and develop better understanding about the economic and social threats to peace, and about the economic and social aspects of other threats, such as terrorism and organized crime;

    (b) We welcome the recent improvement in the exchange of information between the Economic and Social Council and the Security Council, for example through regular meetings of their Presidents, and encourage both bodies to regularize these exchanges.

277. **Second, it can provide an arena in which States measure their commitments to achieving key development objectives in an open and transparent manner.**

278. **Third, it can provide a regular venue for engaging the development community at the highest level, in effect transforming itself into a "development cooperation forum".** To that end:

    (a) **A new approach should be adopted within the Economic and Social Council agenda, replacing its current focus on administrative issues and programme coordination with a more focused agenda built around the major themes contained in the Millennium Declaration;**

    (b) **A small executive committee, comprising members from each regional group, should be created in order to provide orientation and direction to its work and its interaction with principal organs, agencies and programmes;**

    (c) **The annual meetings between the Economic and Social Council and the Bretton Woods institutions should be used to encourage collective action in support of the Millennium Development Goals and the Monterrey Consensus;**

(d) **The Economic and Social Council, with inputs from its secretariat and the United Nations Development Group, should aim to provide guidance on development cooperation to the governing boards of the United Nations funds, programmes and agencies;**

(e) **The Economic and Social Council should provide strong support for the efforts of the Secretary-General and the United Nations Development Group to strengthen the coherence of United Nations action at the field level and its coordination with the Bretton Woods institutions and bilateral donors.**

279. We believe the time has arrived to reconsider the manner of and quantity of funding for the United Nations agencies, funds and programmes. New initiatives in this regard have been explored recently and deserve the special attention of the international community.

Achieving policy coherence

280. While the strategies above are important for a better functioning Economic and Social Council, we appreciate that historical developments in the governance of the multilateral system have limited the capacity of that body to influence international policies in trade, finance and investment. There still remains a need for a body that brings together the key developed and developing countries to address the critical interlinkages between trade, finance, the environment, the handling of pandemic diseases and economic and social development. To be effective, such a body must operate at the level of national leaders.

281. While the annual meetings of the G8 group at head of State or Government level fulfil some of the characteristics required to give greater coherence and impetus to the necessary policies, it would be helpful to have a larger forum bringing together the heads of the major developed and developing countries. One way of moving forward may be to transform into a leader's group the G20 group of finance ministers, which currently brings together States collectively encompassing 80 per cent of the world's population and 90 per cent of its economic activity, with regular attendance by the International Monetary Fund, World Bank, WTO and the European Union. In such meetings, we recommend the inclusion in the group of the Secretary-General of the United Nations and the President of the Economic and Social Council to ensure strong support for United Nations programmes and initiatives.

XVIII. The Commission on Human Rights

282. One of the central missions of the United Nations is to protect human rights, a mission reaffirmed by the Millennium Declaration. The Commission on Human

Rights is entrusted with promoting respect for human rights globally, fostering international cooperation in human rights, responding to violations in specific countries and assisting countries in building their human rights capacity.

283. In recent years, the Commission's capacity to perform these tasks has been undermined by eroding credibility and professionalism. Standard-setting to reinforce human rights cannot be performed by States that lack a demonstrated commitment to their promotion and protection. We are concerned that in recent years States have sought membership of the Commission not to strengthen human rights but to protect themselves against criticism or to criticize others. The Commission cannot be credible if it is seen to be maintaining double standards in addressing human rights concerns.

284. Reform of this body is therefore necessary to make the human rights system perform effectively and ensure that it better fulfils its mandate and functions. We support the recent efforts of the Secretary-General and the United Nations High Commissioner for Human Rights to ensure that human rights are integrated throughout the work of the United Nations, and to support the development of strong domestic human rights institutions, especially in countries emerging from conflict and in the fight against terrorism. Member States should provide full support to the Secretary General and the High Commissioner in these efforts.

285. In many ways, the most difficult and sensitive issue relating to the Commission on Human Rights is that of membership. In recent years, the issue of which States are elected to the Commission has become a source of heated international tension, with no positive impact on human rights and a negative impact on the work of the Commission. Proposals for membership criteria have little chance of changing these dynamics and indeed risk further politicizing the issue. Rather, **we recommend that the membership of the Commission on Human Rights be expanded to universal membership.** This would underscore that all members are committed by the Charter to the promotion of human rights, and might help to focus attention back on to substantive issues rather than who is debating and voting on them.

286. In the first half of its history, the Commission was composed of heads of delegation who were key players in the human rights arena and who had the professional qualifications and experience necessary for human rights work. Since then this practice has lapsed. We believe it should be restored, and we propose that **all members of the Commission on Human Rights designate prominent and experienced human rights figures as the heads of their delegations.**

287. In addition, we propose that **the Commission on Human Rights be supported in its work by an advisory council or panel.** This council or panel would consist of some 15 individuals, independent experts (say, three per region),

appointed for their skills for a period of three years, renewable once. They would be appointed by the Commission on the joint proposal of the Secretary-General and the High Commissioner. In addition to advising on country-specific issues, the council or panel could give advice on the rationalization of some of the thematic mandates and could itself carry out some of the current mandates dealing with research, standard-setting and definitions.

288. **We recommend that the High Commissioner be called upon to prepare an annual report on the situation of human rights worldwide.** This could then serve as a basis for a comprehensive discussion with the Commission. The report should focus on the implementation of all human rights in all countries, based on information stemming from the work of treaty bodies, special mechanisms and any other sources deemed appropriate by the High Commissioner.

289. The Security Council should also more actively involve the High Commissioner in its deliberations, including on peace operations mandates. We also welcome the fact that the Security Council has, with increasing frequency, invited the High Commissioner to brief it on country-specific situations. We believe that this should become a general rule and that **the Security Council and the Peacebuilding Commission should request the High Commissioner to report to them regularly about the implementation of all human rights-related provisions of Security Council resolutions, thus enabling focused, effective monitoring of these provisions.**

290. More also needs to be done with respect to the funding situation of the Office of the High Commissioner. We see a clear contradiction between a regular budget allocation of 2 per cent for this Office and the obligation under the Charter of the United Nations to make the promotion and protection of human rights one of the principal objectives of the Organization. There is also a need to redress the limited funding available for human rights capacity-building. Member States should seriously review the inadequate funding of this Office and its activities.

291. In the longer term, Member States should consider upgrading the Commission to become a "Human Rights Council" that is no longer subsidiary to the Economic and Social Council but a Charter body standing alongside it and the Security Council, and reflecting in the process the weight given to human rights, alongside security and economic issues, in the Preamble of the Charter.

XIX. The Secretariat

292. A strong Secretary-General at the head of a more professional and better organized Secretariat is an essential component of any effective system for collective security in the twenty-first century.

A. Strengthening support for the Secretary-General

293. The creation of the post of Deputy Secretary-General in 1996 helped bring far greater coherence to the work of the United Nations in the economic, social and development fields and on issues of management reform. Given the enormous increase in the workload of the Secretary-General in the area of peace and security in the 1990s, creating a second Deputy Secretary-General post for peace and security would ensure that the Secretary-General's efforts in this area are equally well supported. **To assist the Secretary-General, an additional Deputy Secretary-General position should be created, responsible for peace and security.**

294. With one Deputy Secretary-General focusing on the economic and social development work of the United Nations, the additional Deputy Secretary-General and his/her office would assist the Secretary-General in systematically overseeing the work of the United Nations system in the area of peace and security, with the aim of formulating integrated strategies and ensuring concerted action. Such an office should not be operational and would not duplicate, but instead rationalize and make more effective, existing bureaucratic functions. It would integrate inputs from the various departments and agencies and prepare early-warning reports and strategy options for decision by the Secretary-General. It should comprise approximately 15 Professionals able to perform strategic analysis, planning and coordination tasks. It should also provide the Secretary-General with new expertise to deal with new threats - for example, the scientific advice necessary to address questions of environmental and biological security.

B. A competent and professional Secretariat

295. The burden of implementing the decisions of Member States and providing them with timely analysis and advice rests not only on the Secretary-General but on the Secretariat as a whole. If the United Nations is to be effective, it needs a professional and well-trained Secretariat whose skills and experiences have been adapted to match the tasks at hand. The last 15 years have witnessed a large expansion in work related to conflict prevention and peacekeeping, the negotiation and implementation of peace agreements, and peacebuilding. And yet, despite the increase in demand since the end of the cold war total Secretariat staff has declined since 1990, while only 6 per cent of the staff of the Secretariat are responsible for the entire range of issues that include mediation, the organization and management of peacekeeping operations, support for the Security Council, disarmament, elections support and sanctions. Many of those based at Headquarters have no field experience or training and the existing rules militate

against their gaining it. In addition, there is little or no expertise for tackling many of the new or emerging threats addressed in the present report.

296. The Secretary-General should be provided with the resources he requires to do his job properly and the authority to manage his staff and other resources as he deems best. To meet the needs identified in the present report, we recommend that:

(a) Member States recommit themselves to Articles 100 and 101 of the Charter of the United Nations;

(b) Member States review the relationship between the General Assembly and the Secretariat with the aim of substantially increasing the flexibility provided to the Secretary-General in the management of his staff, subject always to his accountability to the Assembly;

(c) The Secretary-General's reform proposals of 1997 and 2002 related to human resources should now, without further delay, be fully implemented;

(d) There should be a one-time review and replacement of personnel, including through early retirement, to ensure that the Secretariat is staffed with the right people to undertake the tasks at hand, including for mediation and peacebuilding support, and for the office of the Deputy Secretary-General for peace and security. Member States should provide funding for this replacement as a cost-effective long-term investment;

(e) The Secretary-General should immediately be provided with 60 posts - less than 1 per cent of the total Secretariat - for the purpose of establishing all the increased Secretariat capacity proposed in the present report.

XX. The Charter of the United Nations

297. Our recommendations on Security Council reform will require the amendment of Article 23 of the Charter of the United Nations. In addition, we suggest the following modest changes to the Charter:

298. **Articles 53 and 107 (references to enemy States) are outdated and should be revised** – revisions should be appropriately drafted to avoid retroactively undermining the legal provisions of these articles. The Charter should reflect the hopes and aspirations of today, not the fears of 1945.

299. **Chapter 13 (The Trusteeship Council) should be deleted.** The Trusteeship Council of the United Nations performed an important task in helping the world emerge from the era of colonialism and steering many cases of successful

decolonization. The United Nations should turn its back on any attempt to return to the mentalities and forms of colonialism.

300. **Article 47 (The Military Staff Committee) should be deleted, as should all references to the body in Articles 26, 45 and 46.** It is no longer appropriate for the joint chiefs of staff of the five permanent members to play the role imagined for them in 1945. We have in paragraph 258 above addressed the need for the Security Council to have better military advice.

301. We believe, however, that the Charter as a whole continues to provide a sound legal and policy basis for the organization of collective security, enabling the Security Council to respond to threats to international peace and security, both old and new in a timely and effective manner. The Charter was also farsighted in its recognition of the dependence of international peace and security on economic and social development.

302. **All Member States should rededicate themselves to the purposes and principles of the Charter and to applying them in a purposeful way, matching political will with the necessary resources. Only dedicated leadership within and between States will generate effective collective security for the twenty-first century and forge a future that is both sustainable and secure.**

Annexes

Annex I

Summary of recommendations

Note: The number in parentheses that appears after each summarized recommendation refers to the paragraph in the main report that contains the complete text of the recommendation.

Contents

Part 1
Collective security and the challenge of prevention

Poverty, infectious disease and environmental degradation

1. All States must recommit themselves to the goals of eradicating poverty, achieving sustained economic growth and promoting sustainable development. (59)

2. The many donor countries which currently fall short of the United Nations 0.7 per cent gross national product target for official development assistance should establish a timetable for reaching it. (60)

3. World Trade Organization members should strive to conclude the Doha development round of multilateral trade negotiations at the latest in 2006. (62)

4. Lender Governments and the international financial institutions should provide highly indebted poor countries with greater debt relief, longer rescheduling and improved access to global markets. (63)

5. Although international resources devoted to meeting the challenge of HIV/AIDS have increased from about $250 million in 1996 to about $2.8 billion in 2002, more than $10 billion annually is needed to stem the pandemic. (64)

6. Leaders of countries affected by HIV/AIDS need to mobilize resources, commit funds and engage civil society and the private sector in disease-control efforts. (65)

7. The Security Council, working closely with UNAIDS, should host a second special session on HIV/AIDS as a threat to international peace and security, to explore the future effects of HIV/AIDS on States and societies, generate research on the problem and identify critical steps towards a long-term strategy for diminishing the threat. (67)

8. International donors, in partnership with national authorities and local civil society organizations, should undertake a major new global initiative to rebuild local and national public health systems throughout the developing world. (68)

9. Members of the World Health Assembly should provide greater resources to the World Health Organization Global Outbreak Alert and Response Network to increase its capacity to cope with potential disease outbreaks. (69)

10. States should provide incentives for the further development of renewable energy sources and begin to phase out environmentally harmful subsidies, especially for fossil fuel use and development. (71)

11. We urge Member States to reflect on the gap between the promise of the Kyoto Protocol and its performance, re-engage on the problem of global warming and begin new negotiations to produce a new long-term strategy for reducing global warming beyond the period covered by the Protocol (2012). (72)

Conflict between and within States

12. The Security Council should stand ready to use the authority it has under the Rome Statute to refer cases of suspected war crimes and crimes against humanity to the International Criminal Court. (90)

13. The United Nations should work with national authorities, international financial institutions, civil society organizations and the private sector to develop norms governing the management of natural resources for countries emerging from or at risk of conflict. (92)

14. The United Nations should build on the experience of regional organizations in developing frameworks for minority rights and the protection of democratically elected Governments from unconstitutional overthrow. (94)

15. Member States should expedite and conclude negotiations on legally binding agreements on the marking and tracing, as well as the brokering and transfer, of small arms and light weapons. (96)

16. All Member States should report completely and accurately on all elements of the United Nations Register of Conventional Arms, and the Secretary-General should be asked to report annually to the General Assembly and Security Council on any inadequacies in the reporting. (97)

17. A training and briefing facility should be established for new or potential special representatives of the Secretary-General and other United Nations mediators. (101)

18. The Department of Political Affairs should be given additional resources and should be restructured to provide more consistent and professional mediation support. (102)

19. While the details of such a restructuring should be left to the Secretary-General, it should take into account the need for the United Nations to have:

   (a) A field-oriented, dedicated mediation support capacity, comprised of a small team of professionals with relevant direct experience and expertise, available to all United Nations mediators;

   (b) Competence on thematic issues that recur in peace negotiations, such as the sequencing of implementation steps, the design of monitoring arrangements, the sequencing of transitional arrangements and the design of national reconciliation mechanisms;

(c) Greater interaction with national mediators, regional organizations and non-governmental organizations involved in conflict resolution;

(d) Greater consultation with and involvement in peace processes of important voices from civil society, especially those of women, who are often neglected during negotiations. (103)

20. National leaders and parties to conflict should make constructive use of the option of preventive deployment of peacekeepers. (104)

Nuclear, radiological, chemical and biological weapons

21. The nuclear-weapon States must take several steps to restart disarmament:

(a) They must honour their commitments under Article VI of the Treaty on the Non-Proliferation of Nuclear Weapons to move towards disarmament and be ready to undertake specific measures in fulfilment of those commitments;

(b) They should reaffirm their previous commitments not to use nuclear weapons against non-nuclear-weapon States. (120)

22. The United States and the Russian Federation, other nuclear-weapon States and States not party to the Treaty on the Non-Proliferation of Nuclear Weapons should commit to practical measures to reduce the risk of accidental nuclear war, including, where appropriate, a progressive schedule for de-alerting their strategic nuclear weapons. (121)

23. The Security Council should explicitly pledge to take collective action in response to a nuclear attack or the threat of such attack on a non-nuclear weapon State. (122)

24. Negotiations to resolve regional conflicts should include confidence-building measures and steps towards disarmament. (123)

25. States not party to the Treaty on the Non-Proliferation of Nuclear Weapons should pledge a commitment to non-proliferation and disarmament, demonstrating their commitment by ratifying the Comprehensive Nuclear-Test-Ban Treaty and supporting negotiations for a fissile material cut-off treaty, both of which are open to nuclear-weapon and non-nuclear-weapon States alike. We recommend that peace efforts in the Middle East and South Asia launch nuclear disarmament talks that could lead to the establishment of nuclear-weapon-free zones in those regions similar to those established for Latin America and the Caribbean, Africa, the South Pacific and South-East Asia. (124)

26. All chemical-weapon States should expedite the scheduled destruction of all existing chemical weapons stockpiles by the agreed target date of 2012. (125)

27.	States parties to the Biological and Toxin Weapons Convention should without delay return to negotiations for a credible verification protocol, inviting the active participation of the biotechnology industry. (126)

28.	The Board of Governors of the International Atomic Energy Agency (IAEA) should recognize the Model Additional Protocol as today's standard for IAEA safeguards, and the Security Council should be prepared to act in cases of serious concern over non-compliance with non-proliferation and safeguards standards. (129)

29.	Negotiations should be engaged without delay and carried forward to an early conclusion on an arrangement, based on the existing provisions of Articles III and IX of the IAEA statute, which would enable IAEA to act as a guarantor for the supply of fissile material to civilian nuclear users. (130)

30.	While that arrangement is being negotiated, States should, without surrendering the right under the Treaty on the Non-Proliferation of Nuclear Weapons to construct uranium enrichment and reprocessing facilities, voluntarily institute a time-limited moratorium on the construction of any further such facilities, with a commitment to the moratorium matched by a guarantee of the supply of fissile materials by the current suppliers at market rates. (131)

31.	All States should be encouraged to join the voluntary Proliferation Security Initiative. (132)

32.	A State's notice of withdrawal from the Treaty on the Non-Proliferation of Nuclear Weapons should prompt immediate verification of its compliance with the Treaty, if necessary mandated by the Security Council. The IAEA Board of Governors should resolve that, in the event of violations, all assistance provided by IAEA should be withdrawn. (134)

33.	The proposed timeline for the Global Threat Reduction Initiative to convert highly enriched uranium reactors and reduce HEU stockpiles should be halved from 10 to five years. (135)

34.	States parties to the Biological and Toxin Weapons Convention should negotiate a new bio-security protocol to classify dangerous biological agents and establish binding international standards for the export of such agents. (137)

35.	The Conference on Disarmament should move without further delay to negotiate a verifiable fissile material cut-off treaty that, on a designated schedule, ends the production of highly enriched uranium for non-weapon as well as weapons purposes. (138)

36.	The Directors-General of IAEA and the Organization for the Prohibition of Chemical Weapons should be invited by the Security Council to report to it twice-yearly on the status of safeguards and verification processes, as well as on any serious concerns they have which might fall short of an actual breach of the

Treaty on the Non-Proliferation of Nuclear Weapons and the Chemical Weapons Convention. (140)

37. The Security Council should consult with the Director-General of the World Health Organization to establish the necessary procedures for working together in the event of a suspicious or overwhelming outbreak of infectious disease. (144)

Terrorism

38. The United Nations, with the Secretary-General taking a leading role, should promote a comprehensive strategy against terrorism, including:

     (a) Dissuasion, working to reverse the causes or facilitators of terrorism, including through promoting social and political rights, the rule of law and democratic reform; working to end occupations and address major political grievances; combating organized crime; reducing poverty and unemployment; and stopping State collapse;

     (b) Efforts to counter extremism and intolerance, including through education and fostering public debate;

     (c) Development of better instruments for global counter-terrorism cooperation, all within a legal framework that is respectful of civil liberties and human rights, including in the areas of law enforcement; intelligence-sharing, where possible; denial and interdiction, when required; and financial controls;

     (d) Building State capacity to prevent terrorist recruitment and operations;

     (e) Control of dangerous materials and public health defence. (148)

39. Member States that have not yet done so should actively consider signing and ratifying all 12 international conventions against terrorism, and should adopt the eight Special Recommendations on Terrorist Financing issued by the Organization for Economic Cooperation and Development (OECD)-supported Financial Action Task Force on Money-Laundering and the measures recommended in its various best practices papers. (150)

40. The Al-Qaida and Taliban Sanctions Committee should institute a process for reviewing the cases of individuals and institutions claiming to have been wrongly placed or retained on its watch lists. (152)

41. The Security Council, after consultation with affected States, should extend the authority of the Counter-Terrorism Executive Directorate to act as a clearing house for State-to-State provision of military, police and border control assistance for the development of domestic counter-terrorism capacities. (154)

42. To help Member States comply with their counter-terrorism obligations, the United Nations should establish a capacity-building trust fund under the Counter-Terrorism Executive Directorate. (155)

43. The Security Council should devise a schedule of predetermined sanctions for State non-compliance with the Council's counter-terrorism resolutions. (156)

44. The General Assembly should rapidly complete negotiations on a comprehensive convention on terrorism, incorporating a definition of terrorism with the following elements:

    (a) recognition, in the preamble, that State use of force against civilians is regulated by the Geneva Conventions and other instruments, and, if of sufficient scale, constitutes a war crime by the persons concerned or a crime against humanity;

    (b) restatement that acts under the 12 preceding anti-terrorism conventions are terrorism, and a declaration that they are a crime under international law; and restatement that terrorism in time of armed conflict is prohibited by the Geneva Conventions and Protocols;

    (c) reference to the definitions contained in the 1999 International Convention for the Suppression of the Financing of Terrorism and Security Council resolution 1566 (2004);

    (d) description of terrorism as "any action, in addition to actions already specified by the existing conventions on aspects of terrorism, the Geneva Conventions and Security Council resolution 1566 (2004), that is intended to cause death or serious bodily harm to civilians or non-combatants, when the purpose of such act, by its nature or context, is to intimidate a population, or to compel a Government or an international organization to do or to abstain from doing any act". (163-4)

Transnational organized crime

45. Member States that have not signed, ratified or resourced the 2000 United Nations Convention against Transnational Organized Crime and its three Protocols, and the 2003 United Nations Convention against Corruption should do so, and all Member States should support the United Nations Office on Drugs and Crime in its work in this area. (172)

46. Member States should establish a central authority to facilitate the exchange of evidence among national judicial authorities, mutual legal assistance among prosecutorial authorities and the implementation of extradition requests. (173)

47. A comprehensive international convention on money-laundering that addresses the issues of bank secrecy and the development of financial havens needs to be negotiated, and endorsed by the General Assembly. (174)

48. Member States should sign and ratify the Protocol to Prevent, Suppress and Punish Trafficking in Persons, Especially Women and Children, and parties to the Protocol should take all necessary steps to effectively implement it. (175)

49. The United Nations should establish a robust capacity-building mechanism for rule-of-law assistance. (177)

The role of sanctions

50. The Security Council must ensure that sanctions are effectively implemented and enforced:

    (a) When the Security Council imposes a sanctions regime - including arms embargoes - it should routinely establish monitoring mechanisms and provide them with the necessary authority and capacity to carry out high-quality, in-depth investigations. Adequate budgetary provisions must be made to implement those mechanisms;

    (b) Security Council sanctions committees should be mandated to develop improved guidelines and reporting procedures to assist States in sanctions implementation, and to improve procedures for maintaining accurate lists of individuals and entities subject to targeted sanctions;

    (c) The Secretary-General should appoint a senior official with sufficient supporting resources to enable the Secretary-General to supply the Security Council with analysis of the best way to target sanctions and to assist in coordinating their implementation. This official would also assist compliance efforts; identify technical assistance needs and coordinate such assistance; and make recommendations on any adjustments necessary to enhance the effectiveness of sanctions;

    (d) Donors should devote more resources to strengthening the legal, administrative, and policing and border-control capacity of Member States to implement sanctions. Capacity-building measures should include efforts to improve air-traffic interdiction in zones of conflict;

    (e) The Security Council should, in instances of verified, chronic violations, impose secondary sanctions against those involved in sanctions-busting;

    (f) The Secretary-General, in consultation with the Security Council, should ensure that an appropriate auditing mechanism is in place to oversee sanctions administration. (180)

51. Sanctions committees should improve procedures for providing humanitarian exemptions and routinely conduct assessments of the humanitarian impact of sanctions. The Security Council should continue to strive to mitigate the humanitarian consequences of sanctions. (181)

52. Where sanctions involve lists of individuals or entities, sanctions committees should establish procedures to review the cases of those claiming to have been incorrectly placed or retained on such lists. (182)

Part 3
Collective security and the use of force

Using force: rules and guidelines

53.   Article 51 of the Charter of the United Nations should be neither rewritten nor reinterpreted, either to extend its long-established scope (so as to allow preventive measures to non-imminent threats) or to restrict it (so as to allow its application only to actual attacks). (192)

54.   The Security Council is fully empowered under Chapter VII of the Charter of the United Nations to address the full range of security threats with which States are concerned. The task is not to find alternatives to the Security Council as a source of authority but to make the Council work better than it has. (198)

55.   The Panel endorses the emerging norm that there is a collective international responsibility to protect, exercisable by the Security Council authorizing military intervention as a last resort, in the event of genocide and other large-scale killing, ethnic cleansing or serious violations of humanitarian law which sovereign Governments have proved powerless or unwilling to prevent. (203)

56.   In considering whether to authorize or endorse the use of military force, the Security Council should always address - whatever other considerations it may take into account - at least the following five basic criteria of legitimacy:

(a)   *Seriousness of threat.* Is the threatened harm to State or human security of a kind, and sufficiently clear and serious, to justify *prima facie* the use of military force? In the case of internal threats, does it involve genocide and other large-scale killing, ethnic cleansing or serious violations of international humanitarian law, actual or imminently apprehended?

(b)   *Proper purpose.* Is it clear that the primary purpose of the proposed military action is to halt or avert the threat in question, whatever other purposes or motives may be involved?

(c)   *Last resort.* Has every non-military option for meeting the threat in question been explored, with reasonable grounds for believing that other measures will not succeed?

(d)   *Proportional means.* Are the scale, duration and intensity of the proposed military action the minimum necessary to meet the threat in question?

(e)   *Balance of consequences.* Is there a reasonable chance of the military action being successful in meeting the threat in question, with the consequences of action not likely to be worse than the consequences of inaction? (207)

57. The above guidelines for authorizing the use of force should be embodied in declaratory resolutions of the Security Council and General Assembly. (208)

Peace enforcement and peacekeeping capability

58. The developed States should do more to transform their existing force capacities into suitable contingents for peace operations. (216)

59. Member States should strongly support the efforts of the Department of Peacekeeping Operations, building on the important work of the Panel on United Nations Peace Operations of the United Nations Secretariat, to improve its use of strategic deployment stockpiles, standby arrangements, trust funds and other mechanisms in order to meet the tighter deadlines necessary for effective deployment. (218)

60. States with advanced military capacities should establish standby high readiness, self-sufficient battalions at up to brigade level that can reinforce United Nations missions, and should place them at the disposal of the United Nations. (219)

61. The Secretary-General should recommend and the Security Council should authorize troop strengths for peacekeeping missions that are sufficient to deter and repel hostile factions. (222)

62. The United Nations should have a small corps of senior police officers and managers (50-100 personnel) who could undertake mission assessments and organize the start-up of police components of peace operations, and the General Assembly should authorize this capacity. (223)

Post-conflict peacebuilding

63. Special representatives of the Secretary-General should have the authority and guidance to work with relevant parties to establish robust donor-coordinating mechanisms, as well as the resources to perform coordination functions effectively, including ensuring that the sequencing of United Nations assessments and activities is consistent with Government priorities. (226)

64. The Security Council should mandate and the General Assembly should authorize funding for disarmament and demobilization programmes from assessed budgets for United Nations peacekeeping operations. (227)

65. A standing fund for peacebuilding should be established at the level of at least $250 million that can be used to finance the recurrent expenditures of a nascent Government, as well as critical agency programmes in the areas of rehabilitation and reintegration. (228)

Protecting civilians

66. All combatants must abide by the Geneva Conventions. All Member States should sign, ratify and act on all treaties relating to the protection of civilians, such as the Genocide Convention, the Geneva Conventions, the Rome Statute of the International Criminal Court and all refugee conventions. (233)

67. The Security Council should fully implement resolution 1265 (1999) on the protection of civilians in armed conflict. (237)

68. The Security Council, United Nations agencies and Member States should fully implement resolution 1325 (2000) on women, peace and security. (238)

69. Member States should support and fully fund the proposed Directorate of Security and accord high priority to assisting the Secretary-General in implementing a new staff security system in 2005. (239)

Part 4
A more effective United Nations
for the twenty-first century

The General Assembly

70. Members of the General Assembly should use the opportunity provided by the Millennium Review Summit in 2005 to forge a new consensus on broader and more effective collective security. (240)

71. Member States should renew efforts to enable the General Assembly to perform its function as the main deliberative organ of the United Nations. This requires a better conceptualization and shortening of the agenda, which should reflect the contemporary challenges facing the international community. Smaller, more tightly focused committees could help to sharpen and improve resolutions that are brought to the whole Assembly. (242)

72. Following the recommendation of the report of the Panel on Eminent Persons on United Nations-Civil Society Relations, the General Assembly should establish a better mechanism to enable systematic engagement with civil society organizations. (243)

The Security Council

73. Reforms of the Security Council should meet the following principles:

    (a) They should, in honouring Article 23 of the Charter of the United Nations, increase the involvement in decision-making of those who contribute most to the United Nations financially, militarily and diplomatically - specifically in terms of contributions to United Nations assessed budgets, participation in mandated peace operations, contributions to the voluntary activities of the United Nations in the areas of security and development, and diplomatic activities in support of United Nations objectives and mandates. Among developed countries, achieving or making substantial progress towards the internationally agreed level of 0.7 per cent of gross national product for official development assistance should be considered an important criterion of contribution;

    (b) They should bring into the decision-making process countries more representative of the broader membership, especially of the developing world;

    (c) They should not impair the effectiveness of the Security Council;

    (d) They should increase the democratic and accountable nature of the body. (249)

74.   A decision on the enlargement of the Council, satisfying these criteria, is now a necessity. The presentation of two clearly defined alternatives, of the kind described below as models A and B, should help to clarify - and perhaps bring to resolution - a debate which has made little progress in the last 12 years. (250)

75.   Models A and B both involve a distribution of seats as between four major regional areas, which we identify, respectively, as "Africa", "Asia and Pacific", "Europe" and "Americas". We see these descriptions as helpful in making and implementing judgements about the composition of the Security Council, but make no recommendation about changing the composition of the current regional groups for general electoral and other United Nations purposes. Some members of the Panel, in particular our Latin American colleagues, expressed a preference for basing any distribution of seats on the current regional groups. (251)

76.   Model A provides for six new permanent seats, with no veto being created, and three new two-year term non-permanent seats, divided among the major regional areas. Model B provides for no new permanent seats, but creates a new category of eight four-year renewable-term seats and one new two-year non-permanent (and non-renewable) seat, divided among the major regional areas. (252-253)

77.   In both models, having regard to Article 23 of the Charter, a method of encouraging Member States to contribute more to international peace and security would be for the General Assembly, taking into account established practices of regional consultation, to elect Security Council members by giving preference for permanent or longer-term seats to those States that are among the top three financial contributors in their relevant regional area to the regular budget, or the top three voluntary contributors from their regional area, or the top three troop contributors from their regional area to United Nations peacekeeping missions. (254)

78.   There should be a review of the composition of the Security Council in 2020, including, in this context, a review of the contribution (as defined in paragraph 249 of the main report) of permanent and non-permanent members from the point of view of the Council's effectiveness in taking collective action to prevent and remove new and old threats to international peace and security. (255)

79.   The Panel recommends that under any reform proposal, there should be no expansion of the veto. (256)

80.   A system of "indicative voting" should be introduced, whereby members of the Security Council could call for a public indication of positions on a proposed action. (257)

81.   Processes to improve transparency and accountability in the Security Council should be incorporated and formalized in its rules of procedure. (258)

A Peacebuilding Commission

82. The Security Council, acting under Article 29 of the Charter of the United Nations and after consultation with the Economic and Social Council, should establish a Peacebuilding Commission. (263)

83. The core functions of the Peacebuilding Commission should be to identify countries that are under stress and risk sliding towards State collapse; to organize, in partnership with the national Government, proactive assistance in preventing that process from developing further; to assist in the planning for transitions between conflict and post-conflict peacebuilding; and in particular to marshal and sustain the efforts of the international community in post-conflict peacebuilding over whatever period may be necessary. (264)

84. While the precise composition, procedures and reporting lines of the Peacebuilding Commission will need to be established, they should take account of the following guidelines:

    (a) The Peacebuilding Commission should be reasonably small;
    (b) It should meet in different configurations, to consider both general policy issues and country-by-country strategies;
    (c) It should be chaired for at least one year and perhaps longer by a member approved by the Security Council;
    (d) In addition to representation from the Security Council, it should include representation from the Economic and Social Council;
    (e) National representatives of the country under consideration should be invited to attend;
    (f) The Managing Director of the International Monetary Fund, the President of the World Bank and, when appropriate, heads of regional development banks should be represented at its meetings by appropriate senior officials;
    (g) Representatives of the principal donor countries and, when appropriate, the principal troop contributors should be invited to participate in its deliberations;
    (h) Representatives of regional and subregional organizations should be invited to participate in its deliberations when such organizations are actively involved in the country in question. (265)

85. A Peacebuilding Support Office should be established in the Secretariat to give the Peacebuilding Commission appropriate Secretariat support and to ensure that the Secretary-General is able to integrate system-wide peacebuilding policies and strategies, develop best practices and provide cohesive support for field operations. (266)

Regional organizations

86. In relation to regional organizations:

    (a) Authorization from the Security Council should in all cases be sought for regional peace operations;

    (b) Consultation and cooperation between the United Nations and regional organizations should be expanded and could be formalized in an agreement, covering such issues as meetings of the heads of the organizations, more frequent exchange of information and early warning, co-training of civilian and military personnel, and exchange of personnel within peace operations;

    (c) In the case of African regional and subregional capacities, donor countries should commit to a 10-year process of sustained capacity-building support, within the African Union strategic framework;

    (d) Regional organizations that have a capacity for conflict prevention or peacekeeping should place such capacities in the framework of the United Nations Standby Arrangements System;

    (e) Member States should agree to allow the United Nations to provide equipment support from United Nations-owned sources to regional operations, as needed;

    (f) The rules for the United Nations peacekeeping budget should be amended to give the United Nations the option on a case-by-case basis to finance regional operations authorized by the Security Council with assessed contributions. (272)

The Economic and Social Council

87. The Economic and Social Council should provide normative and analytical leadership in a time of much debate about the causes of, and interconnections between, the many threats we face. To that end, the Economic and Social Council should establish a Committee on the Social and Economic Aspects of Security Threats. (276)

88. The Economic and Social Council should provide an arena in which States measure their commitments to achieving key development objectives in an open and transparent manner. (277)

89. The Economic and Social Council should provide a regular venue for engaging the development community at the highest level, in effect transforming itself into a "development cooperation forum". To that end:

(a) A new approach should be adopted within the Economic and Social Council agenda, replacing its current focus on administrative issues and programme coordination with a more focused agenda built around the major themes contained in the Millennium Declaration;

(b) A small executive committee, comprising members from each regional group, should be created in order to provide orientation and direction to the work of the Economic and Social Council and its interaction with principal organs, agencies and programmes;

(c) The annual meetings between the Economic and Social Council and the Bretton Woods institutions should be used to encourage collective action in support of the Millennium Development Goals and the Monterrey Consensus;

(d) The Economic and Social Council, with inputs from its secretariat and the United Nations Development Group, should aim to provide guidance on development cooperation to the governing boards of the United Nations funds, programmes and agencies;

(e) The Economic and Social Council should provide strong support to the efforts of the Secretary-General and the United Nations Development Group to strengthen the coherence of United Nations action at the field level and its coordination with the Bretton Woods institutions and bilateral donors. (278)

The Commission on Human Rights

90. Membership of the Commission on Human Rights should be made universal. (285)

91. All members of the Commission on Human Rights should designate prominent and experienced human rights figures as the heads of their delegations. (286)

92. The Commission on Human Rights should be supported in its work by an advisory council or panel. (287)

93. The United Nations High Commissioner for Human Rights should be called upon to prepare an annual report on the situation of human rights worldwide. (288)

94. The Security Council and the Peacebuilding Commission should request the High Commissioner for Human Rights to report to them regularly on the implementation of all human rights-related provisions of Security Council resolutions, thus enabling focused, effective monitoring of those provisions. (289)

The Secretariat

95. To assist the Secretary-General, an additional Deputy Secretary-General position should be created, responsible for peace and security. (293)

96. The Secretary-General should be provided with the resources he requires to do his job properly and the authority to manage his staff and other resources as he deems best. To meet the needs identified in the present report, the Panel recommends that:

   (a) Member States recommit themselves to Articles 100 and 101 of the Charter of the United Nations;

   (b) Member States review the relationship between the General Assembly and the Secretariat with the aim of substantially increasing the flexibility provided to the Secretary-General in the management of his staff, subject always to his accountability to the Assembly;

   (c) The Secretary-General's reform proposals of 1997 and 2002 related to human resources should now, without further delay, be fully implemented;

   (d) There should be a one-time review and replacement of personnel, including through early retirement, to ensure that the Secretariat is staffed with the right people to undertake the tasks at hand, including for mediation and peacebuilding support, and for the office of the Deputy Secretary-General for peace and security. Member States should provide funding for this replacement as a cost-effective long-term investment;

   (e) The Secretary-General should immediately be provided with 60 posts – less than 1 per cent of the total Secretariat capacity – for the purpose of establishing all the increased Secretariat capacity proposed in the present report. (296)

The Charter of the United Nations

97. In addition to any amendment of Article 23 of the Charter of the United Nations required by proposed reform of the Security Council, the Panel suggests the following modest changes to the Charter:

98. Articles 53 and 107 (references to enemy States) are outdated and should be revised. (298)

99. Chapter XIII (The Trusteeship Council) should be deleted. (299)

100. Article 47 (The Military Staff Committee) should be deleted, as should all references to the Committee in Articles 26, 45 and 46. (300)

101. All Member States should rededicate themselves to the purposes and principles of the Charter and to applying them in a purposeful way, matching political will

with the necessary resources. Only dedicated leadership within and between States will generate effective collective security for the twenty-first century and forge a future that is both sustainable and secure. (302)

Annex II
Panel members and terms of reference

Members

Anand **Panyarachun**, Chair (Thailand)

Former Prime Minister of Thailand

Robert **Badinter** (France)

Member of the French Senate and former Minister of Justice of France

João Clemente **Baena Soares** (Brazil)

Former General Secretary of the Ministry of External Relations of Brazil and Secretary-General of the Organization of American States

Gro Harlem **Brundtland** (Norway)

Former Prime Minister of Norway and Director-General of the World Health Organization

Mary **Chinery-Hesse** (Ghana)

Vice-Chairman of the National Development Planning Commission of Ghana and former Deputy Director-General of the International Labour Organization

Gareth **Evans** (Australia)

President of the International Crisis Group and former Minister for Foreign Affairs of Australia

David **Hannay** (United Kingdom)

Former Permanent Representative of the United Kingdom to the United Nations and United Kingdom Special Envoy to Cyprus

Enrique **Iglesias** (Uruguay)	President of the Inter-American Development Bank and former Minister for Foreign Relations of Uruguay
Amre **Moussa** (Egypt)	Secretary-General of the League of Arab States and former Minister for Foreign Affairs of Egypt
Satish **Nambiar** (India)	Former Lt. General in the Indian Army and Force Commander of UNPROFOR
Sadako **Ogata** (Japan)	President of the Japan International Cooperation Agency and former United Nations High Commissioner for Refugees
Yevgeny **Primakov** (Russian Federation)	Former Prime Minister of the Russian Federation
Qian **Qichen** (China)	Former Vice Premier and Minister for Foreign Affairs of China
Nafis **Sadik** (Pakistan)	Special Envoy of the United Nations Secretary-General for HIV/AIDS in Asia and former Executive Director of the United Nations Population Fund
Salim Ahmed **Salim** (United Republic of Tanzania)	Former Prime Minister of the United Republic of Tanzania and Secretary-General of the Organization of African Unity
Brent **Scowcroft** (United States)	Former Lt. General, United States Air Force and United States National Security Adviser

Terms of reference

1. The past year has shaken the foundations of collective security and undermined confidence in the possibility of collective responses to our common problems and challenges. It has also brought to the fore deep divergences of opinion on the range and nature of the challenges we face and are likely to face in the future.

2. The aim of the High-level Panel on Threats, Challenges and Change is to recommend clear and practical measures for ensuring effective collective action, based upon a rigorous analysis of future threats to peace and security, an appraisal of the contribution collective action can make and a thorough assessment of existing approaches, instruments and mechanisms, including the principal organs of the United Nations.

3. The Panel is not being asked to formulate policies on specific issues, nor on the role of the United Nations in specific places. Rather, it is being asked to provide a new assessment of the challenges ahead and to recommend the changes which will be required if these challenges are to be met effectively through collective action.

4. Specifically, the Panel will:

   (a) Examine today's global threats and provide an analysis of future challenges to international peace and security. While there may continue to exist a diversity of perception on the relative importance of the various threats facing particular Member States on an individual basis, it is important to find an apropriate balance at the global level. It is also important to understand the connections between different threats;

   (b) Identify clearly the contribution that collective action can make in addressing these challenges;

   (c) Recommend the changes necessary to ensure effective collective action, including but not limited to a review of the principal organs of the United Nations.

5. The Panel's work is confined to the field of peace and security, broadly interpreted. That is, it should extend its analysis and recommendations to other issues and institutions, including economic and social ones, to the extent that they have a direct bearing on future threats to peace and security.

Annex III

Panel secretariat

Stephen **Stedman** (Research Director)

Loraine **Rickard-Martin** (Secretary to the Panel)

Bruce **Jones** (Deputy Research Director)

Muhammad Zeeshan **Amin**

Tarun **Chhabra**

Sebastian Graf von **Einsiedel**

Angela **Irving**

Graham **Maitland**

Angelica **Malic**

Thant **Myint-U**

Maria **Zaroui**

Annex IV

Panel meetings, regional consultations and issue workshops

Panel meetings

Date and place

5-7 December 2003 Princeton, United States of America	16-18 July 2004 Baden, Austria
13-15 February 2004 Mont Pelerin, Switzerland	24-26 September 2004 Tarrytown, United States of America
30 April-2 May 2004 Addis Ababa, Ethiopia	3-5 November 2004 New York City, United States of America

Regional consultations and issue workshops

Date (2004) and place	*Meeting/theme*	*Organizer*
13-14 January Harriman, United States of America	"The Secretary-General's High-level Panel: maximizing prospects for success"	Stanley Foundation
29 January New York City, United States of America	Briefing to NGOs on United Nations reform initiatives and the High-level Panel	Department of Public Information of the United Nations Secretariat
16 February Paris, France	Meeting of the High-level Panel with the Parliamentary Assembly of the Council of Europe	Parliamentary Assembly of the Council of Europe

Date (2004) and place	Meeting/theme	Organizer
23-25 February West Sussex, United Kingdom	"Addressing contemporary security threats: what role for the United Nations?"	Wilton Park
27 February New Haven, United States of America	"Security Council reform"	Yale Center for the Study of Globalization
1 March Stanford, United States of America	"Nuclear proliferation"	Stanford University Center for International Security and Cooperation
1 and 2 March Harriman	"Use of force"	Stanley Foundation and United Nations Foundation
2 and 3 March Harriman	"Intervention in humanitarian crises"	Stanley Foundation and United Nations Foundation
4 March New York City	"Terrorism and non-State actors"	Stanley Foundation, United Nations Foundation and Ralph Bunche Institute of International Studies
5 March New York City	"The future of the weapons of mass destruction regimes"	Government of New Zealand and International Peace Academy

Date (2004) and place	Meeting/theme	Organizer
7 and 8 March Rio de Janeiro, Brazil	Regional consultations	Viva Rio and New York University Center on International Cooperation
12-14 March 26-27 March Manhasset, United States of America	Retreat for permanent representatives and Panel members to discuss the work of the High-level Panel	Governments of Australia, Mexico, the Netherlands, Singapore and South Africa, and International Peace Academy
18-20 March Oslo, Norway	Regional consultations	Norwegian Institute for International Affairs and New York University Center on International Cooperation
28-30 March Geneva, Switzerland	Workshop on Article 51 of the Charter of the United Nations and future threats to international security	Government of Switzerland
29 and 30 March Harriman	"Small arms and light weapons"	Stanley Foundation and United Nations Foundation
2-4 April Hangzhou, China	Asia High-level Symposium on Threats, Challenges and Change	Government of China
5 April Cambridge, United States of America	"Nuclear arms control and proliferation"	Harvard University Belfer Center for Science and International Affairs, Nuclear Threat Initiative and United Nations Foundation

Date (2004) and place	Meeting/theme	Organizer
8 April New York City	Outreach to humanitarian and human rights NGOs	Friedrich Ebert Stiftung and United Nations Foundation
16 and 17 April Stanford	"Governance and sovereignty"	Stanford Institute for International Studies
19 April Washington D.C., United States of America	"Bio-security"	United States National Academies of Sciences, Nuclear Threat Initiative and United Nations Foundation
21-24 April Singapore	"Dialogue on security in Asia: concepts, threats and assurances after 9/11"	Singapore Institute for International Affairs and New York University Center on International Cooperation
25-27 April Shanghai, China	Meeting on the work of the High-level Panel at the sixtieth session of Economic and Social Commission for Asia and the Pacific (ESCAP)	Economic and Social Commission for Asia and the Pacific
27-29 April Addis Ababa, Ethiopia	Regional consultations	Inter-Africa Group and New York University Center on International Cooperation

Date (2004) and place	Meeting/theme	Organizer
30 April Addis Ababa	High-level meeting with the Commission of the African Union	High-level Panel secretariat and Bureau of the Chairperson of the African Union
2 May Addis Ababa	Meeting with African civil society organizations	High-level Panel secretariat
6 May New York City	Outreach to civil society, economic and social development NGOs	Friedrich Ebert Stiftung and United Nations Foundation
10 and 11 May Warrenton, United States of America	"Development, poverty and security"	Stanley Foundation and United Nations Foundation
13 and 14 May Washington D.C.	Conference on Security Council change	Johns Hopkins University Institute for Transatlantic Relations
17-19 May Mexico City, Mexico	"Governance, democracy and free markets"	Instituto Tecnológico Autónomo de México, Friedrich Ebert Stiftung and United Nations Foundation
21-23 May Cape Town, South Africa	"The United Nations, regional organizations and future security threats in Africa"	Center for Conflict Resolution, Friedrich Ebert Stiftung and United Nations Foundation

Date (2004) and place	Meeting/theme	Organizer
24 and 25 May Warsaw, Poland	"New threats, new responses"	Government of Poland
27-29 May Rome, Italy	"The United Nations and new threats: rethinking security"	Istituto Affari Internazionali, Aspen Institute Italia, Istituto Italiano per l'Africa e l'Oriente, United Nations Foundation and United Nations Interregional Crime and Justice Research Institute
2 June Washington D.C.	"Environment and security"	Woodrow Wilson International Center for Scholars and United Nations Foundation
8 and 9 June Copenhagen, Denmark	"Strengthening United Nations capacity for crisis management"	Government of Denmark
11-16 June Prouts Neck, United States of America	Thirty-ninth Conference on the United Nations for the Next Decade	Stanley Foundation
17 and 18 June London, United Kingdom	"Poverty and security: an integrated approach"	London School of Economics and Political Science, United Kingdom Department of International Development and United Nations Foundation

Date (2004) and place	Meeting/theme	Organizer
28 and 29 June Oxford, United Kingdom	"Security for the billion at the bottom"	Oxford University and Stanford Institute for International Studies
1-3 July New Delhi, India	"United Nations and the new threats: rethinking security"	Institute of Peace and Conflict Studies and United Nations Foundation
6 and 7 July Kyoto, Japan	"Threats, challenges and change: internal violence"	Government of Japan
11 and 12 September Cairo, Egypt	"Threats, challenges and reform: building security in the Mediterranean and Gulf region"	Egyptian Council for Foreign Affairs, Al-Ahram Center for Political and Strategic Studies, United Nations Foundation, Friedrich Ebert Stiftung, Istituto Affari Internazionali